DUN

IN TI

1550–1700

Following the sudden closure of the Augustinian Priory in the mid-sixteenth century, Dunstable's businessmen, retailers, traders and commuters needed to work together for change and eventually effected a very successful recovery.

Then came the Civil War and all groups suffered financial loss and some individuals serious distress. However, once the war was over, travellers started to pass through the town and the people took every opportunity to build up new businesses and to turn Dunstable into one of the leading travel centres between London and Holyhead.

Situated on two main roads they were in an excellent position to exploit this vibrant new industry. However, it also meant that they were exposed to the gossip, sedition, discussions and secret meetings which took place. The fate of kings, bishops and the Church of England were argued about in Dunstable's many inns. So it is not surprising that a second theme weaves in and out of these chapters; the struggle for freedom of worship. Some of the first Baptists in this country were a breakaway movement from the Priory Church of St. Peter and the early Quakers were welcomed at a house near the crossroads.

The 17th century has been described as 'a century of change' and Dunstable was at the centre of these enormous upheavals. This book opens to an uncertain future, covers the hardships and distress of war, follows the story of the town's newly found prosperity and leaves it on the brink of even greater success and security.

A very detailed street scene of High Street North, drawn by Thomas Rowlandson (1756–1827). (Courtesy: The Trustees, The Cecil Higgins Art Gallery, Bedford.)

Confirmation that The Lyon and The Peacock really did stand in the middle of the road. A stage coach outside The White Hart, a private coach outside The Sugar Loaf and a group of ladies begging.

Shows the importance of the two ponds; a blacksmith's forge to the north. The inn sign reads 'The Crown Posting House'.

DUNSTABLE

IN TRANSITION

1550–1700

Vivienne Evans

The Book Castle

This book is the second in a series on the History of Dunstable since 1100. The first volume is entitled 'Dunstable with the Priory, 1100–1550'

First published November 1998
by
The Book Castle
12 Church Street
Dunstable
Bedfordshire LU5 4RU

ISBN 1 871199 98 0

Cover: Rear view of the Red Lion (corner of Church Street and High Street North) in a painting of September 1860 by James Paul André.

Computer typeset by Keyword, Aldbury, Herts.
Printed in Great Britain by Antony Rowe, Chippenham, Wilts.

ABOUT THE AUTHOR

Vivienne Evans is one of Bedfordshire's most experienced history lecturers and authors. In addition to leading dozens of local history courses, she has also written numerous books and booklets including Dunstable with the Priory, 1100–1550; History All Around; John Bunyan, his life and times; Folk, characters and events in the History of Bedfordshire and Northamptonshire; the Dunstable Swan Jewel; Chronicle featuring Middle Row; The Book of Dunstable and Houghton Regis; and Falkes de Breauté and the Siege of Bedford Castle. She also runs a tourism and research organisation called Dunstable Historic and Heritage Studies.

AUTHOR'S ACKNOWLEDGEMENTS

The publication of this book has been greatly delayed by family illness which has involved typing, retyping and constant corrections. The willpower to continue has been provided by the extreme patience, support and encouragement of our publisher, Paul Bowes, the interest in Dunstable's history and heritage shown by Richard Walden and members of the Dunstable Town Council, the great loyalty shown by the committee and the students who attend courses put on by the Workers' Educational Association, Sheila Furnell and Bob Sutton who are encouraging coach parties to visit our beautiful Priory Church and the numerous people who have stopped me in the street to ask when this book will appear. The staff at the County Record Office, [now Bedfordshire and Luton Archives and Records Service] have helped to trace many of the references used and we are particularly grateful to those people who have allowed us to use their photographs and drawings.

Marlene Pothecary once more typed most of the original version and our daughter Rosamond and friend Adele Kane took time off work to rush through the final version.

This proud and exciting period of Dunstable's history has not been previously available under one cover and we are grateful to all the people who have helped us to get it finished.

CREDITS TO PICTURES

BM	British Museum
DTC	Dunstable Town Council
MD	Produced for Moore's of Dunstable by Countryside Arts
RD	Roderick Davies
LPE	Lewis Evans
FAF	Alec Fowler
EH	Ernie Hawes
AL	Andrew Leach
JL	John Lunn
BM	Brenda Mills
OR	Omer Roucoux

I would like to thank the above for permission to use their drawings and photographs. Also the owners of the Five Bells at Stanbridge for the drawings from their menu, Dunstable Town Council for the use of a drawing which they commissioned from Bernard West and Luton Borough Council for allowing us to photograph two coaches from their important collection.

The Gregorian Calendar

When using dates it must be remembered that in 1752 there was a major change in the British system of recording them. Up until then the 'year' had begun on March 25th, but when Britain adopted the Gregorian Calendar it began on January 1st. This sometimes leads to apparent inaccuracies. Where possible the dates in this book have been adapted to the New Style of recording.

CONTENTS

INTRODUCTION

The first book in this series[1] ended with the closure of the Augustinian Priory, which had dominated the town for well over 400 years. The prior, or his representative, had been not only spiritual leader of the residents but also their landlord, the owner and administrator of their market and fairs, the owner and controller of their manor court and had stood in the position of sheriff when more serious crimes had to be judged, or when the king's itinerant justices came into Bedfordshire.

In January 1540 the last prior, Gervase Markham, moved into a cottage in High Street South, with a pension of £60 per year. The canons, who had received much smaller pensions, mainly moved away to take up vacant church livings. Some of them married.

The Honour of Ampthill

All the other churches that the Priory owned, their shops, inns, and houses in Dunstable and their farmland across Bedfordshire, together with all other ex-monastic land in the county, were transferred to what became a great scattered estate, known as the 'Honour' of Ampthill[2]. It was administered originally from offices at Ampthill Castle. Some items on this rent list were sold very quickly, some were let out on long term leases but some, including a large part of Dunstable, remained Crown property until the mid 19th century.

The Change of Administration

One major Crown appointment, which must have smoothed the administrative changes in Dunstable, was that of Adam Hilton as bailiff. Previously bailiff to Gervase Markham, he was well

---

1 Evans, V. Dunstable With the Priory, 1100–1550.

2 Bedfordshire Historical Record Society [BHRS] Vols. 63 & 64.

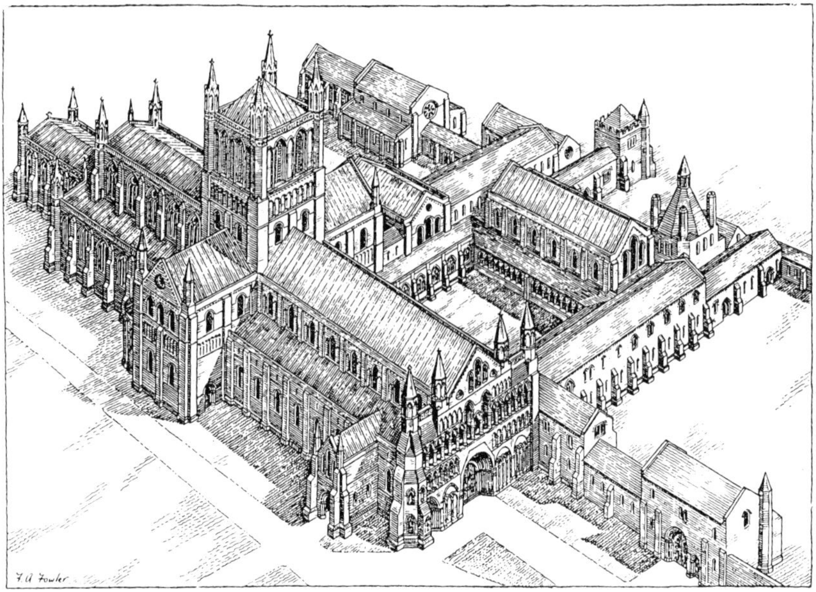

A conjectural view of the Priory Church. (FAF)

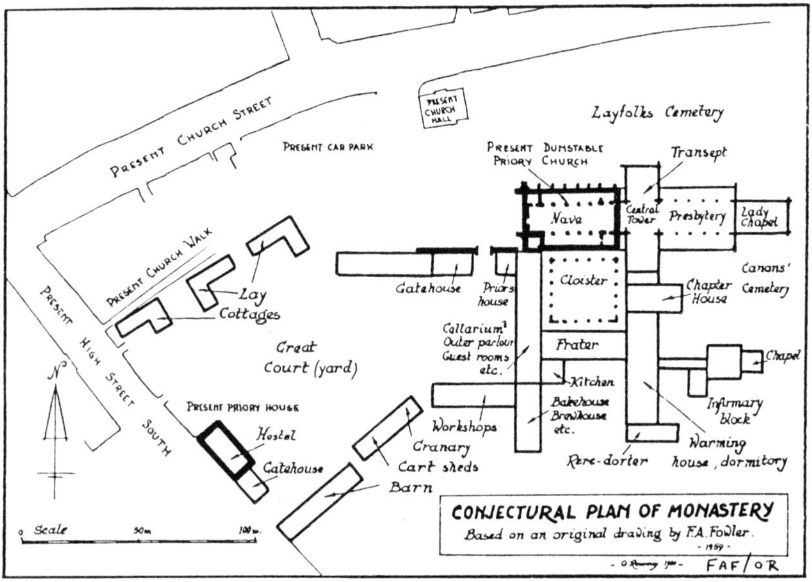

CONJECTURAL PLAN OF MONASTERY
Based on an original drawing by F.A. Fowler. - 1959 -

known and respected by the businessmen of the town. It seems likely that it took some years before the Priory buildings were completely demolished and also likely that the change in administration took place over several years.

Over the centuries the Priory had lost much of its power over its tenants. In 1550 the town, which in the 1220s had witnessed the great struggle between the businessmen and Prior Richard de Morins, was economically much the same as when King Henry I founded it soon after 1100. It was an important centre of merchants dealing in corn, hides and fleeces. Not only did these merchants rent farms in the surrounding villages but they also bought in raw materials from other farmers on the Chiltern Hills and across South Bedfordshire. They sorted, cleaned, graded and re-packed these products before arranging export deals or sending them off to fairs, or to manufacturers, in other parts of the country. Also, because of the presence of these merchants, the town's position on the crossing of two main roads, the numerous pilgrims who visited the Shrine of St. Fremund, and other visitors to the Priory, Dunstable became a very successful retail centre. This probably continued, but national trends altered and, as other market towns caught up with Dunstable's success, the business centre changed. Wholesaling and the import–export business became largely centred on the City of London, but Dunstable was saved by its advantageous roads. It became an ideal country centre for commuting businessmen to live in and perhaps establish their offices.

The Fraternity of St. John The Baptist

When in 1442, several of the leading businessmen applied to King Henry VI for a licence to found a fraternity, several of these commuters were involved. This fraternity was intended to provide enough money to employ a chaplain to recite masses for the souls of the brethren and also to provide a school, possibly for their own sons, plus accommodation for their elderly members and for travellers. When the Priory closed, there was no mention of the canons running a school or an almshouse, but there was reference to 'a schoolhouse' in South Street and to property which the Fraternity owned in West Street. Adjacent to the latter was a house, rented to the 'Guardians of the Parish' for 3 shillings (15p) per year. It seems likely therefore, that long before the Dissolution, the Fraternity had already taken over some of the responsibilities previously held by the Priory.

As Adam Hilton, the bailiff, was himself a member of the Fraternity, he could no doubt call on other members to help him convince the prior on matters of long-term planning and on the day-to-day running of the town. If so, when Gervase Markham moved out of the Priory and Hilton's employer became the king's representative at Ampthill, he could expect the members to help him with the re-organisation.

However, in 1547, King Edward VI, the young son of Henry VIII, closed down these fraternities, on the grounds that private masses had no place in his new, Protestant, Church of England. When their houses and property passed to the king, regular meetings were no longer held[3]. Nevertheless the continuing presence of the former administrative structure of the Fraternity, i.e. those men who had once held office, meant that there was, living in and around the town, a hierarchy used to taking control and making decisions; also the other residents must have been accustomed, willingly or unwillingly, to accept their control*.

The owner of the White Horse, Thomas Bentley, was sometimes described as 'Yeoman of the Crown', the tenant of the White Hart was John Fayre, and by 1541 Adam Hilton was tenant of the Saracen's Head. These men all belonged to the Fraternity and as the story of Dunstable unfolds we will find that unofficial leaders of the business community were mainly innkeepers. However, the national problems which increased rapidly after the Dissolution, such as the care of the roads and the care of the unemployed, aged and sick, were, in Queen Mary's reign, made the responsibility of the parish.

---

3 Brown, J.E. Chantry Certificates for Bedfordshire.

* Figures quoted when the Fraternity was closed suggest Dunstable had a population of about 500 but calculations below show this figure to be much too low

Law and Order

Minor offences were still handled, within the town, by the Manor Court, but the king's itinerant judges no longer visited Dunstable and all major offenders were sent to the sheriff at Bedford. During the first year, i.e. 1540, before the residents had understood what the changes really meant, one of the tenants caused a local problem and was forcibly evicted by men sent into the town by the sheriff. The town constable was so concerned about this violent behaviour that he officially ordered the men making the eviction to keep the peace and was supported by one or two of the other residents. However the sheriff, who must have decided that a show of authority was important now that Dunstable was at last in his jurisdiction, had the constable and his supporters put in the stocks! Later they were transferred to Bedford gaol.

The Destruction of the Priory Buildings

Although the Dominican Friary had been surrendered in May 1534, four and a half years went by before Bishop Ingworth of Dover arrived to 'recover' the house for the king. Despite the fact that Thomas Bentley's tenancy agreement had excluded the bells and all the lead on the site, except that used in the gutter and drains, the Bishop recorded that 'of the goods . . . some were sold, some stolen and some pledged . . .' before his arrival. [There could just be a connection in that the earliest recorded name for the recently renovated, timber-framed building, number 16–18 West Street, was 'The Leaden Porch'.]

In most cases, the signing of the documents transferring religious houses to the Crown, was followed, as quickly as possible, by the arrival of an official, such as the Bishop of Dover. He was expected to supervise the removal of all the lead and the precious objects and send them for safe keeping to the Tower of London. He, or another official, then had to witness the removal of the church roof, the breaking up of the bells into moveable-sized metal pieces, the start of the destruction of the buildings and if possible to arrange a local sale of the stone.

Nos. 16–18 West Street. For many years an inn, once known as the 'Leaden Porch'. (JH)

Nos. 16–18 West Street after a storm in 1986 brought down part of the chimney. (LPE)

However, it seems unlikely that this procedure was carried out at the Priory. This was because of King Henry VIII's plan, c1540, to use the magnificent church [10 feet/3 metres higher and three times longer than the present building] as the centre for a new diocese. Only after a long delay did these plans fall through and destruction take place. Even then the part of the church used by the towns' people was saved. This is now known as The Priory Church of St. Peter.

Priory House

In some towns the purchaser of the monastic hostel was expected to convert it to an inn. As Dunstable already had so many inns this may not have applied. Because of the delay it was put into the care of Richard Greenway, Usher of the King's Chamber. He was described as 'Keeper' of the 'mansion, chief messuage and gardens'[4]. If we take mansion and messuage together it could mean Priory House and the great courtyard with its barns, stables and other buildings, plus the gardens. This would cover today's Priory House and gardens. The Priory buildings *may* have still been standing on what is now Priory Meadow.

During the reign of Queen Mary the house and grounds were transferred to Sir Leonard Chamberlain. He had held many administrative positions in Buckinghamshire and the surrounding counties during the reigns of both King Henry and his son Edward, and he supported Queen Mary's claim to the throne. She knighted him, the day after her coronation, and a few months later granted him Priory House, the site of the Priory, and other land in Bedfordshire.

Plans for the new bishopric had long since been forgotten and the time had come to sell all the old buildings. A committee of local businessmen, including Henry Bevell* and Richard Denton (in 1542 tenant of the Lyon inn and a great deal of other property) bought the estate and held it for seven years until they sold it to Richard and Elizabeth Aves. The story of Priory House will continue in a later chapter.

4 Victoria County History [VCH] Bedfordshire, Vol. 3.
* (see page 10)

The Southern side of the Priory Church with a small area of the Priory meadow which covers and protects the ruins of the Priory. In the foreground the Manshead Archaeological Society are excavating on the site of an old hedge which had been removed. This area was once the courtyard of the Priory. (LPE)

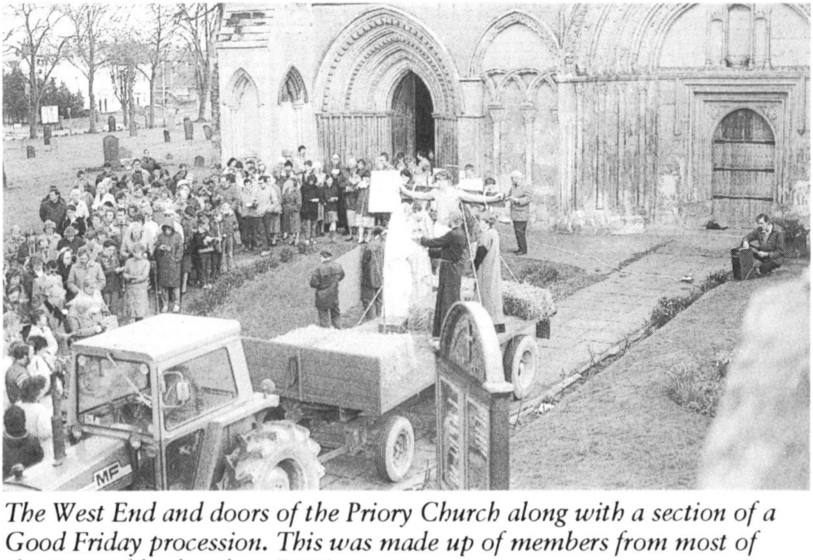

The West End and doors of the Priory Church along with a section of a Good Friday procession. This was made up of members from most of the Dunstable churches. (LPE)

The East End of the Priory Church infilled after the removal of the monastic buildings. (FAF)

Inside the East End of the church, showing the blocked off arches once used as entrances to the Canon's part of the church. (FAF)

Conjectural drawing by Bernard West of the rood screen and the wall which separated the town church from the area used by the canons. (DTC)

(from page 7)

* The spelling is 'Bevell' but it may well have been Henry Bennell. The 1542 rent list includes a 'John Benolles' as tenant of the Peacock, which stood next to the Lyon, in the middle of High Street North. At a later date the inn is referred to as 'Bennell's House' (see below).

The back of Middle Row, before restoration, showing repairs, carried out some centuries ago, with re-used monastic stone. (EH)

The Old Palace of Kingsbury

In 1204, King John had given the royal palace to the Priory and from then on royal parties stayed at the prior's private lodging house.

In a deed of 1130/31 granting the town of Dunstable to the Priory, King Henry I described his 'houses of the town and the garden where I am wont to entertain'. Nearly a hundred years later, in 1227, when King Henry III confirmed the gift of King John, he described it as 'all that site and garden where King Henry grandfather of King Henry our father once had houses in Dunstable before the cemetery of the Church of the Blessed Peter, towards the north . . .'. In a later sentence it orders that the Prior and Canons should 'have and hold the said garden and site to build for themselves or dispose of for themselves as they please . . .'.

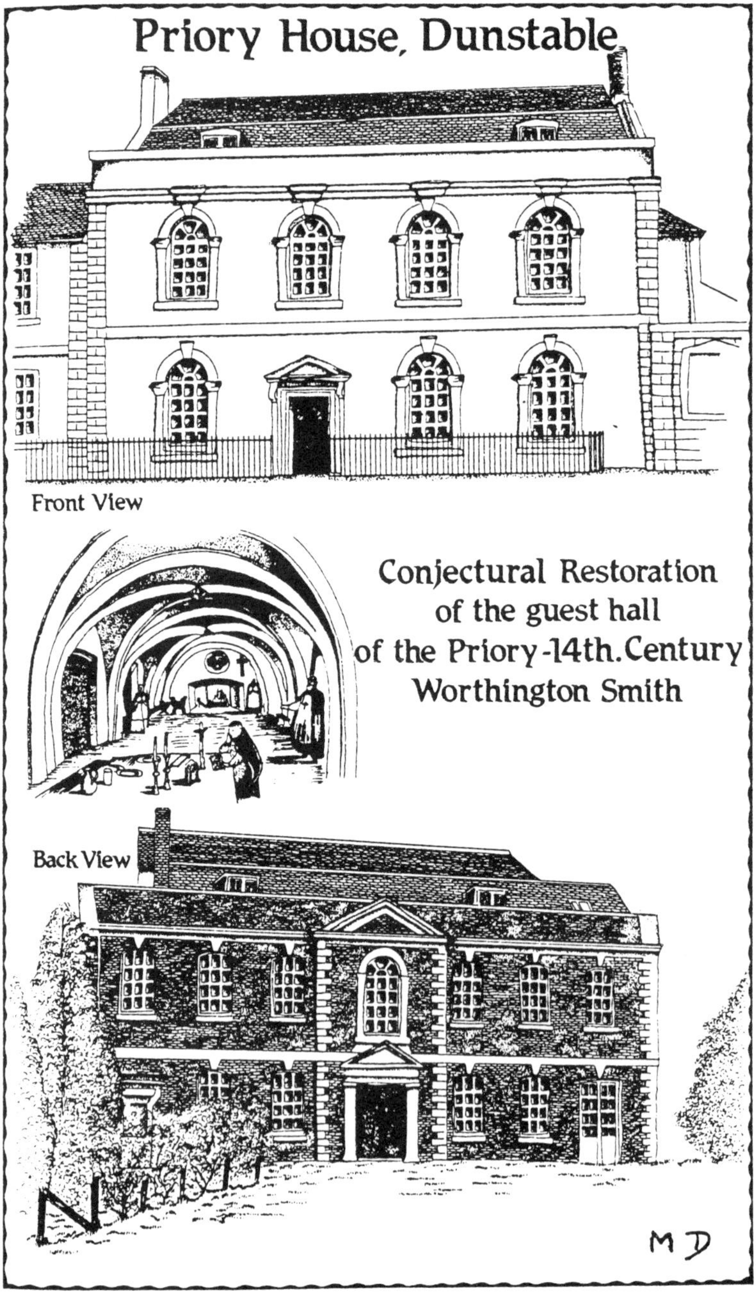
Priory House, Dunstable
Front View
Conjectural Restoration
of the guest hall
of the Priory-14th.Century
Worthington Smith
Back View
MD

There is evidence that at first the prior *may* have let out the old palace to the extremely wealthy businessman, John Durrant, and that after his death it was in a very bad state of repair. Wylie, in his account of England during the reign of King Henry IV, records that Henry stayed at the old royal palace of Kingsbury on the night of November 3rd 1405 on the way back from fighting in Wales[5]. It was over 100 years later before the Priory was closed; in 1542 it was not included in the Priory property transferred to the Honour of Ampthill. However, George Cavendish, friend and biographer of Sir Thomas Wolsey, rented land and property all around Kingsbury and is referred to as owning the principal house on Church Street. He definitely bought the church land of neighbouring Houghton Regis and, as Wolsey and his friends sometimes bought monastic property before the Dissolution, he may have bought the Kingsbury estate before 1540[6]. In 1525 he was President of the Dunstable Fraternity.

The next time Kingsbury is referred to in the records is in the 17th century, when it is the home of William Marsh (see below).

The Problems Caused by Religion in the Late 16th Century

Despite the terrible things which happened in some parts of England, there is no evidence that there was any bitter controversy in Dunstable. Men and women born in the early years of Henry VIII's reign took it for granted that they would accept the Roman Catholic form of service and the control, some might say interference, of the Pope. Back in 1414, some Dunstablians had become involved in a revolt against practices approved of by the Pope. This movement, known as Lollardy, was brutally brought to an end, but as more and more people began to read the Bible, the difference between the teaching of

---

5 Wylie, J.H. History of England Under Henry IV. Vol. 2.

6 Nicholls, Y. BHRS Vol. 64.

Jesus and the teaching of the medieval church became a subject of secret discussion. Some Dunstablians must have become aware that Martin Luther, a professor of philosophy at Wittenberg University, was preaching against these same practices which had been objected to by the Lollards. An example would be the raising of money for good causes through the sale of 'indulgences' for which the purchaser, it was said, could obtain forgiveness for sins past, present, or future. Secret discussions there may have been but there was no open revolt.

Then, in 1533, the national. religious drama of the day moved to Dunstable. Henry VIII, wanting to marry Anne Boleyn, convinced himself, and some of the English church leaders, that his first marriage, to Catherine of Aragon, had been illegal because he had married his brother's widow. The Pope refused to agree to an annulment so Henry defied him and an English court was set up, at Dunstable Priory, to examine the king's 'great and weighty cause'. They found in the king's favour and this meant a deliberate defiance of the People[7]. Within the next twelve months England was completely separated from the authority of Rome. However, no change of doctrine was permitted until the reign of Edward VI, when the Latin mass-book was superceded by the Book of Common Prayer.

A twenty-year-old, living in Dunstable when the annulment was announced, would only have been forty when Queen Mary came to the throne, and for five years England once again became a Roman Catholic country.

Although Queen Elizabeth was anxious to restore the Reformed religion, she and her ministers tried to make the national church acceptable to the moderates of both sides. However, the doctrine included the undebatable belief that salvation came by faith and faith came from reading the scriptures, and from hearing the scriptures expounded by a Reformed preacher. These preachers had to be ordained by a bishop, use the Book of Common Prayer at every service, wear the clothes prescribed for the purpose, and follow the ritual laid

---

7 Lunn, J. The Priory Church of Saint Peter.

down for the different ceremonies and rites of the church. However, the law that was to cause trouble, in 17th century Dunstable, was that *every adult had to attend their own parish church every Sunday*, whether or not they approved of the service.

By the end of the 16th century a growing number of clergymen were being taken to the church court for various 'offences', such as refusing to wear a surplice or refusing to bow at the altar.

What Happened at the Priory Church of St. Peter

Little is known about what happened at the Priory after 1540. The rectory was leased to the bailiff, Adam Hilton, who would have appointed a vicar to take the services. The 'rector' was an individual, or representative of an organisation, who owned the church land and the great tithes; up until the Dissolution he was often the head of a religious house. However, after the Dissolution, rectorships were leased or sold to the highest bidder. If the new rector was a secular individual, like Adam Hilton, he would appoint a vicar to take the services. If, however, the new rector was an ordained clergyman he could, if he wished, take the services himself.

Early in the reign of Protestant King Edward, *Robert Russel* was appointed *rector* and on 13th November 1554, about a year after Roman Catholic Queen Mary was crowned, the rector was the *Rev. John Cooper*. No leaving date is given for either of them but a *'Mr Collier Minister'*, who was buried on 12th May 1559, may have been appointed by Cooper. Queen Mary died on 17th November 1558 and some time in that year the *Rev. William Walker* became *rector*. He was buried at the Priory Church on 14th March 1585 having ministered at the Priory for the first thirty years of Queen Elizabeth's reign. Unfortunately we do not know what relationship he had with his congregation. His successor, the *Rev. Johannes Barnes*, wasn't installed until 14th January 1588, but the clerical subsidy (tax) for 1586 and 1587 was paid by a James Tydye. He was a major tenant and he, or his son, still rented a house and land in 1624. There are no further references to Barnes who *may* have been appointed by rector James Tydye.

John Richardson BA – Rebel Priest

During the 1570s and 1580s, when William Walker was at the Priory Church, individuals and families from all over Bedfordshire were reported to the church court for infringement of church laws, especially for not attending church. Apart from William Atkinson, who was reported as a common drunkard, Dunstable names do not appear.

No dates are recorded for the arrival, or the departure, of curate *John Richardson*. Maybe he was originally curate for absentee rector Johannes Barnes? The first reference to his presence in Dunstable is an entry in the diocesan records, 18th January 1604. It appears that he was one of a growing number of ministers who did not want services restricted by the Book of Common Prayer and resented the control that distant, very wealthy, bishops held over local church communities.

The court was told that he had already been warned three times for being an unconforming minister, i.e. refusing to wear a surplice, not using the sign of the cross at baptism, nor a ring in marriage*. Presumably he ignored this fourth warning because he was summoned again on 14th November. He may have been told that this was a final warning because he asked for time to consider his position. He was allowed two weeks but failed to appear on 1st December, saying he was too lame to travel. He still did not attend court in January, so at the end of the month he was suspended from his living. He may have consulted the church wardens and his friends in the congregation, because someone must have persuaded him that obstinacy was not the best course of action for himself or for the congregation of the Priory Church.

Three-and-a-half months later, on 15th May 1605, he promised 'that from henceforth he will use the ceremonies and

---

* The problems of these nonconforming ministers are set out in Bell, P. Belief in Bedfordshire.

apparel appointed in the execution of his ministry'[8]. The following February he married Elizabeth Webb, from a family who would soon be identified as one which had extremely Puritanical beliefs. Their first baby was born on 1st July 1607 and they gave her the Old Testament name Triphena, but sadly she was buried ten days later. The following November they had a son, whom they baptised Eubulus. Unfortunately nothing more is known about the Richardson family. It is probable that they left Dunstable.

8 Lincoln Record Society [LRS] Vol. 23.

Chapter 1

Innkeepers, Businessmen and Trades People in the Late 16th Century

The Inns

What saved Dunstable after the closing of the Priory was its position on the crossroads. As we saw in the first book of this series, three years before the Priory closed Henry VIII broke with tradition and stayed at the White Horse Inn. Presumably that is where he stayed when he visited Dunstable in later years.

Queen Elizabeth frequently travelled into and across Bedfordshire but there is no record that she used inns. the Stuart kings also preferred to accept the free hospitality they could receive from the landed gentry. However, every royal visit generated a great number of official visitors on affairs of state, as well as family visits for those courtiers and civil servants who accompanied the royal party[9]. Keeping up standards in anticipation of this type of visitor meant that bishops, judges, and higher government officers would automatically arrange to break their journeys in towns used by royal parties.

Quite apart from this branch of the tourist trade, Dunstable benefitted greatly from its position 35–40 miles from London, Oxford and Cambridge. It was also on the direct route not only from the East Anglian ports to Bristol and the West Coast but also on the direct route from the Kentish ports to the East Midlands – via Hockliffe and Woburn; and to the West Midlands, North-west England, Wales, Ireland, and Western

9 Nichols, J.A. The Progresses of Queen Elizabeth.

Scotland via the Holyhead Road.

Travel was still on foot or horseback unless people were prepared to ride on the very slow, long-distance wagons intended for transporting goods. the roads were atrocious and were still too wet, heavy and potholed in winter, and too deep with hidden potholes and dry powdery dust in summer, to make it worthwhile using coaches. It is said that Queen Elizabeth was given one of the first coaches in this country but that it was so uncomfortable that she wouldn't use it. A replica can be seen in the Mossman Collection, Stockwood Park, Luton. From this, one can appreciate the massive frame that was needed to withstand being dragged across the deeply rutted roads in what is now regarded as central London. Dunstable was in a location which encouraged long distance travellers to stay overnight. Coming through the town from the south, they had to leave via the terrifyingly steep and slippery Puddle Hill. Coming from the north, they had to leave the town along several miles of road overhung with scrub and bushes. The Houghton Regis parish register for March 13th 1574 records that they had buried a young man 'found slayne at Puddell Bridge with his legs bounde and sore wounded upon his hed and face and was named

A replica of Queen Elizabeth's coach which can be seen at the Mossman Collection at Stockwood Park. (LPE)
Courtesy of Luton Borough Council.

at his buriel John'. Although the highwayman with expensive clothes, horse and pistol was mainly connected with the 17th century, highway robbery had long been a serious and frightening problem. All these combined dangers meant that it was inadvisable to travel once it began to get dark and that hazards on either side of the town were better tackled early in the morning after a good night's sleep!

The reason that there were already so many inns before the Priory closed, was that in Dunstable, as in other busy towns, the number of travellers gradually increased until they required more accommodation than the religious houses could provide; so the Priory was obliged to provide or license what eventually became known as 'inns'. By the time that it was closed, the Priory had opened The Saracen's Head and its neighbour, The George, (probably now part of the former) and licensed several others.

The street line of the four roads had long since been taken up but the Priory built, or allowed to be built, an inn which stood out from the Church Street line, making a new corner site and adding to the length of North Street. When it was pulled down, in June 1963, it was known as The Red Lion but when it was built, and for several hundred years afterwards, it was known as The White Swan. Just as the weekly market, in the middle of South Street, had gradually been licensed to become permanent residential shops and workshops (Middle Row), so around 1400 two inns were built in the middle of North Street. These were called The Lyon and The Peacock and they stood there, impeding the traffic, until they were pulled down in 1804.

Whether tanneries were ever allowed in the centre of the town is unknown but certainly the 'acre plots' offered by King Henry I (at one shilling an acre!) had fairly early on been split lengthways, so that each of the North Street properties had the main house and offices on the street line and then had a very long yard surrounded by cottages, workshops, and barns and stables at the back. Once the business of the wholesaling and handling of vast quantities of raw materials moved away from Dunstable, these outbuildings probably stood empty ready for development.

On the eastern side of the road, the Fayrey, or some other, family built The White Hart. The population of Dunstable, which was possibly around 1,000, all lived along the four main roads or, more often around the long back yards. There were about 150 tenants of the Priory, a few owner-occupiers and an unknown but large number of servants and workers*. There were however five non-residential lanes. What became known as White Hart Lane, was at this time simply known as 'A Deep Lane'. Leading back from North Street at an angle towards Kingsbury, in winter this probably acted as an overflow ditch for the pond! Nevertheless, although the White Hart faced the road, it opened into this lane.

Nearly opposite, Thomas Bently, or some earlier family, had built the prestigious White Horse Inn; the gateway still stands today. Other inns are recorded in the rent list of 1543 and there may have been beer houses and small lodging houses in both West Street and Church Street but they had no big inns. This was probably because there was no room at the back for stables and barns.

So although the Prior's lodging house had been pulled down, the hostel (Priory House) had become a private house and the almonry had been replaced by a house in the care of the Guardians of the Parish, the innkeepers were ready not only to take up the extra visitors who would once have stayed at the Priory, but also to expand their trade as would be needed in the future.

In addition, there were plenty of smaller businesses providing accommodation for poorer travellers, and for some years the Priory hospital continued as a privately run concern. However, this section of the Priory's work – the care of destitute, sick and disabled travellers – would eventually cause a very serious burden.

The Businessmen

Apart from the innkeepers trading in Dunstable at the time of the closing of the Priory, there was also a group of extremely prosperous business people. Several of the Fraternity were members of the City Guild companies. Following their death,

---

* A figure of 4.8 is usually accepted as an average family size. This gives a tenant population of 720 plus a large number of others.

The 19th century Anchor beerhouse was part of the previous White Horse Inn. (LPE)

I am grateful to Andrew Leach for drawing this reconstruction of the White Horse Inn.

brasses were erected in the Priory Church, of which three at least have survived. In addition, there may be an even more rare and important memorial to the earlier members of the Fraternity. High in the present roof can be seen medieval wood carvings of twelve men. Examination of photographs of these figures, taken recently by Omer Roucoux, shows that each one is different and that they are secular gentlemen, holding shields. It may be these same gentlemen and their wives, or some other Fraternity members, who can been seen embroidered in the Fayrey Pall (coffin cover). For safety, this is in the Victoria and Albert Museum, where it is currently on display.

John Fayrey and his son, Henry, who can be seen on this pall, and who may have ordered the making of this internationally famous piece of embroidery as a gift for the Fraternity, were

The third figure from the back, on the north side of the Priory Church roof. It was probably made at the end of the 15th century to represent a member of the Fraternity of St. John the Baptist. The shield has the oldest representation of the arms Dunstable. (OR)

The roof figure above the altar, on the north side, representing another member of the Fraternity. (OR)

The Fayrey Pall.

extremely wealthy merchants and haberdashers. Like many of the Dunstable merchants of this period they dealt in wool as well as in similar made-up goods*.

The Brasses

Several of the brasses which were mounted in the Priory Church to commemorate the businessmen, have survived.

The Brass of Lawrence Pygot

Pygot died in 1450. On his fine brass he is wearing his merchant's gown and his merchant's mark is shown on shields at the base of the brass.

The Brass of Thomas Fynche

Thomas Fynche did not die until 1586 and his son Richard lived

---

* For details of the Dunstable Fraternity, the Fayrey Pall and the Medieval Carved Figures, see booklets by Mr John Lunn, on sale at the Priory Church, also articles in recent copies of the Bedfordshire Magazine. These include illustrations, of the carved figures, by Omer Roucoux. For design and workmanship of the pall see Miss Ann Buck, BHRS Vol. XXV.

The Brass of Henry and Agnes Fayrey on the wall of the Priory Church. (RD)

until 1640. The shields on their brass show that they were members of the Merchant Taylors Company. In 1639 Richard and Elizabeth Fynche, together with several Dunstablians, started a group of charities for the care of the poor (see below). Back in August 1607, when a 'widow Finch' was buried, the clerk recorded that she was 'a charitable benefactor to the poore'.

The Brass of Henry and Agnes Fayrey

In his will, John Fayrey referred to himself as: 'mercer and merchant of the Staple at Calais' (one of a handful of export, agents for the crown). Although it was usually the custom to portray men and women in their best clothes around 1516 when Henry Fayrey and his wife Agnes died, it was the fashion to display the dead in their shrouds. The shrouds hang open to allow viewers to see the decomposing bodies. Whereas we would find this very distasteful, at the time it was regarded as a service to those left behind, reminding them to be prepared – death was at hand! It was also intended to illustrate that their souls had ascended to heaven and that their bodies were no longer of any importance. The very large, double-width shrouds discreetly illustrate their wealth.

The Brass of Richard Fynche on display in Dunstable Priory Church. Courtesy: Rector and Church Wardens.

Dunstable Wills

Many local wills of the period had survived and can be found in the County Record Office at Bedford.

The Will of John Fayrey

He made his will eight months after the Priory was closed and asked to be buried, where he was a parishioner, at St. Steven

Coleman, London. But he also asked for a dirge and a mass to be 'said or sung in Dunstable parish church'. Although many of his generous, charitable bequests were to be distributed in London, it is possible that some of the money which was to be distributed to the poor may have been handed out in Dunstable after the funeral mass was held. The bequests were listed as gifts of money, mainly to his London friends, servants and apprentices, but one large gift, to a local 'charity', was to be bestowed on mending 'noyous highe ways from a myle on this side' [of] Dunstable to Hoklif where moste neade shall requier'. We can interpret his financial position by the fact that he left enough money to pay for a 'dinner, in the "Mercers" Hall, for the whole company of mercers'.

Unfortunately, he does not list his 'goods', 'plate' and 'jewels', probably there were far too many, but orders them to be divided amongst various bequests. However, from various statements that he makes, it seems likely that 1/9th of the value was around £100!

The Will of Elizabeth Aulaby

Elizabeth Aulaby, who died in 1537, listed in detail her goods and plate. As widow of businessman Thomas Aulaby, she was able to leave a hoop of gold and several valuable, large pieces of silver; plus 12 silver spoons with 'gilt knots like strawberries' on them, 6 silver spoons with 'the sign of the apostles on them', a salt of silver with 'scallop shells', and a plain piece of silver standing upon 3 lions.

She had owned numerous cooking dishes made of pewter and brass, and amongst a great deal of table ware: a set of '12 platters, 12 dishes and 12 saucers of pewter' plus two more complete sets of 6 pieces and a further set of 4. Her son Richard inherited all the family land in Beds, Bucks, Herts and Yorkshire. She bequeathed generous gifts to the Dominican Friary, where she was to be buried, and 13s 4d 'towards mending the highway called Puggihill [Puddlehill]'. This bequest today would be approximately 67p but in 1537 would have paid one of her dairymaids' wages for over three months![10] Richard 'Audelaby'

10 Munby, L. How Much is that Worth?

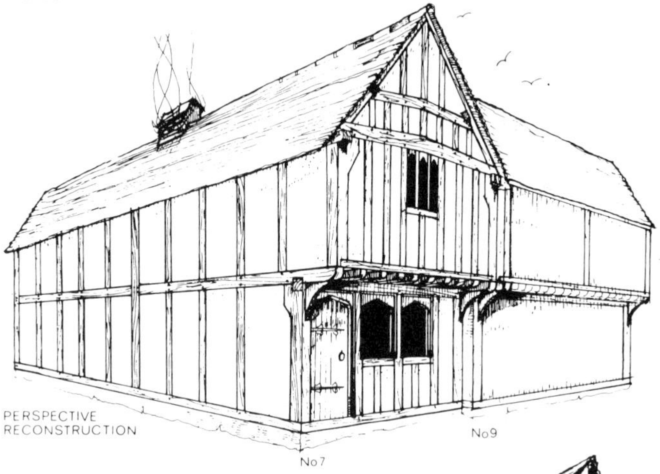

Reconstruction of No. 7 West Street, by John Bailey once Ellis's the barbers and also No. 9 West Street.

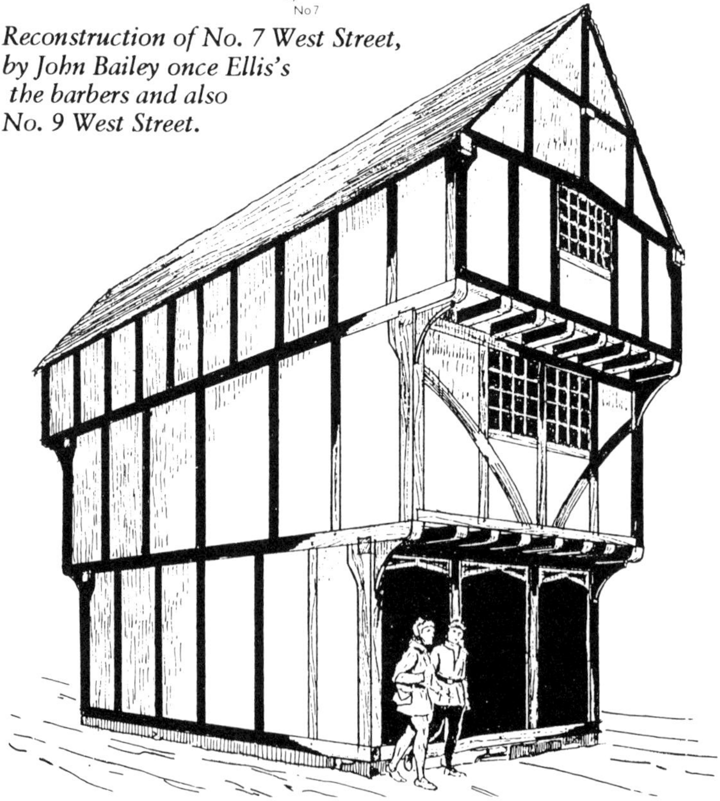

Reconstruction, by John Bailey, of the three-storey shop – workshops in Middle Row.

was one of the largest lease holders, in 1542, in South Street, and had 3 acres of land 'lying under Zouches Hill'. There are also references to land which he owned at the west end of West Street[11].

The Trades People

Well below the social level of the prosperous innkeepers and businessmen, there was a very large group of retailers, beerhouse keepers, craft and tradesmen. Although few of them belonged to the Fraternity, or left memorials in the church, by the standards of the day they lived quite comfortably.

Most of their houses had one big room or hall, where the family lived, cooked on an open fire and slept beside the hearth or behind a screen at the end. However, by 1600 most of them would have had a rough staircase at one end, leading to a private bedroom for the parents, and possibly a ladder at the other end, leading to a 'shelf' of moveable plants. On this, fleeces, rolls of material, old garden tools and apples were stored; a teenage girl who didn't move out into service would end up sleeping 'on the shelf'. At one end of the big hall there would be a screen to separate the food preparation area. This might be called the kitchen but it might also be called the buttery (i.e. bottle area), brewhouse, or if it contained a bolting-ark or tubs, a bolting-house; we would refer to sifting rather than bolting. At a time when poor people's flour was a mixture of 'flour-husk' and bran, to make a reasonable cake or loaf of bread it was necessary to try and remove the latter. As houses improved, so there might be two utility rooms at one end, with one or two bedrooms over them and at the other, a separate parlour, under the bed-chamber.

Families could be large, with three generations made up of elderly or unmarried relations, orphaned nieces and nephews all living together; it meant that inventories include beds in nearly every room. If home-helps, servants or apprentices were employed they might also live in.

---

11 These wills are taken from BHRS Vol. 58.

In cottages there would be no silver and very few pewter vessels but instead wooden trenchers (plates), and baser metal pots, bowls and beakers. Other familiar items were large kettles and poringers, not only for making porridge but for soups and stews and other meals cooked over an open fire. It is possible that some of the poorest cottages were still without a chimney, the smoke finding its way out through a shutter in the roof. However, most of them would soon have a lean-to chimney added at one end. Although some cottages had a built-on oven not all were able to bake food. If there was an oven it was heated by first burning faggots, within the oven; this gave off a very great heat. Items such as bread, needing a very hot oven, went in first to take advantage of the reflected heat, after the ashes had been scraped out; then, as the oven cooled, the bread was replaced by items which required less heat.

Most cooking was done in the pots and pans which hung over the fire, or rested on the fire-irons, but those families who could afford to roast meat turned it over the fire, on a spit. Few of the really poor families left wills but tradespeople, who were a little better off, and lived in the end-terraced cottage, next to the main road, or in between the richer houses along the road, appear to have lived quite comfortably.

Much of the cottage furniture was made at home or by the local carpenter but increasingly the joiner was being employed; so a family would boast of our 'joyned' table or bed. Because so many of life's activities took place in one room, spare space was very short and, where possible, furniture had to be used for more than one purpose, e.g. storage chest-stool, or be able to be packed away. Carpenter-made tables were usually a board, which rested on trestles or boxes, and could be dismantled when not in use.

Because of the expense of jointed chairs and because they took up so much room, they were regarded as a luxury and although there might be one, for the father of the family, or two at the most, the rest of the family sat on forms or stools. Chests and shelves were used for storage and cup-boards were a luxury used for display.

Behind the houses in most towns there were large gardens, paddocks and orchards, and a few humble families were able to rent strips in the common fields. The foundation of Dunstable had provided less than 450 acres of land, so enclosed pieces of 'inland' (within the inner boundary) were mainly rented by the richer families and not many of the cottagers were able to rent strips of agricultural land in the 'outlands'. However, many of the families kept a pig in their back yards.

Inventories

Before a will could be proved an inventory had to be taken. Neighbours helped to value the goods inside and outside the house. They are particularly useful if they identify the separate rooms in the house. Unfortunately, it is not often that both a will and an inventory can be found, but there is a useful collection in the County Record Office. The inventories below are of two middle class Dunstable tradespeople and illustrate the simple but comfortable lifestyle of this important section of the town.

The Inventory of Henry Smith, Tailor

Smith, who was buried on 31 March 1619, had a house facing on to the street (a Henry Smythe had a house and paddock in North Street in 1542). At the back of his house he had a yard with a pigsty and 2 pigs, also a stable with rafters at one end, on which was a supply of hay. HIs inventory was taken twelve days after his death, and mentions the stable but does not include a horse, which may already have been the property of Smith's heir. His will has not survived, but maybe there was a son who had already taken over the family business. There is no inventory of stocks of cloth or of cottons, but a debt is recorded, of £2.13.4d, which may have been for work recently completed. Only richer people used the services of a tailor so maybe, when he was younger, Smith rode around the villages measuring his customers in their own homes and delivering the finished work.

Beside his house was an entrance to his yard and over the

entrance, a small bedroom. Possibly there was a back door into the hall or kitchen, but the front door opened into the parlour; this may originally have been the workshop but by 1619 it had become Smith's bedroom. It contained 'one standinge bedstead, one truckle bedd [which was stored underneath] and the beddinge and other small things there'. These were worth £8.

It was in the hall, a big room open to the roof, that he had his table and cupboard. His 'other joyned and wooden ware' probably included storage chests, which were also used a seats, plus forms and stools. The big open fire was in the hall; his spit and other ironware probably represented the andirons on which the spit rested and shovels and tongs for the care of the fire. Being open to the roof, there would have been no need for a chimney, but over the kitchen was a room with 2 beds and bedding. In the kitchen and hall, i.e. food preparation and eating areas, was brass and pewter worth £6. 'All the sheets and other lynnen about the house' were worth £8 and his clothes were valued at £2.10s.

There was another small bedroom which appears to have been an extension or outhouse, as it is described as 'the room over the seller'. The total value of his possessions was £40.0s.8d.

The Inventory of Elizabeth Ordway, Widow

Elizabeth Ordway, who was buried on 8 May 1619, six weeks after Henry Smith, was also living in a house with a parlour, a hall, one room for the preparation of food and a yard outside but she appears to have had only one bedroom. At her death her heir would have taken over the business but from this inventory of her personal possessions we cannot identify what it was. Her clothes were valued at £3 and her linen at £5.5s.2d. The entire value put on her estate was £152.2s.2d. This was because she was owed £129.14s.6d. If we compare this with Smith's valuation, minus his debts, her inventory valuation is £22.7s.8d compared to his of £37.7s.4d.

Her bed sitting room was over the hall; like Smith she had her standing bed with a 'lowe' bed which could have been stored beneath it. On her bed was a mattress, a featherbed, a bolster, a pair of pillows, 2 blankets and a coverlet. There was also a table, chair, 2 forms and 2 chests. The parlour was partly furnished as a bedroom but also had 3 old chests where the family linen, which included 18 pairs of sheets and 18 napkins, was stored. Put away with her linen were 6 silver spoons.

The one main fireplace was in the hall with: 1 pair andirons (part of the roasting spit), 2 pot-hangers, 1 pair of pot-hooks, 1 gridiron, 1 spit, bellows and tongs. There were also 2 little tables, 9 stools, 2 chairs and a cushion. Her utility room was called a buttery and was well-equipped with brass pots and pans. She had: a pestle and mortar for grinding small quantities of corn or reducing fruit and vegetables to a paste or cream, a ladle, a skimmer and 2 salt-cellars. If people were late coming to the table she had a chafing dish to keep food warm. This was rather like a modern child's double plate, with hot water in the lower one, only wooden embers were used instead of hot water. For use at night she had 4 brass candlesticks, 2 chamber pots and 1 close-stool (commode). No livestock are mentioned and there was nothing of any value in the yard, except wood worth 13s.4d[12].

The Poorer Residents

Despite these examples of the very rich and the comfortably-off, we know from the Hearth Tax in the second half of the 17th century, that a large number of Dunstablians were living below what we would call today 'the poverty line'. The terraces of cottages, which surrounded the big wool and inn yards, were more like hovels.

Although travellers and the numerous inns provided a great deal of skilled and unskilled work, there was, nevertheless, much poverty. This may have been made worse by the shortage of land for growing their own food. The poor may have been tempted to offer accommodation to poor travellers, but it was forbidden. To try to control the spread of disease, and prevent unemployed

12 BHRS Vol. 20.

vagrants adding to the town's problems, the accommodation of strangers was a punishable offence. In 1599 Alice Willet, who was herself both poor and elderly, took pity on a traveller who was 'great with child and so weak and feeble that she could travel no further'. Maybe the distressed woman did become an expense to the community, or maybe Alice's neighbours objected, but someone reported her and she was punished by the church court[13].

In the days of the Priory, poor and sick travellers were attracted to the town by the almonry and the hospital. In 1600 they were still coming. The inns, stables and passing travellers provided so much casual work that there was an underworld of poor, but not starving, families.

Living in Dunstable c1600

Just as there was a big difference in the lifestyles of the two households recorded above and the city businessmen who lived in Dunstable, so there was just as much difference but this time downwards, from the lives of the poor families in the courtyards. Although the very rich probably bought some of their better clothes, furniture and luxury foods in London, there would have been shops in Dunstable able to supply them. Tea, coffee, and chocolate were not yet available but the shops would have been well stocked with a good variety of meats, fish, bread, groceries, fruit, vegetables and luxuries such as imported spices and wine. These shops would also have been patronised by the richer travellers but there must have been many humbler shops for the poor people.

Dunstable was still a busy, prosperous town, able to entertain all types of travellers. There were many poor people but very few, if any, residents who were actually destitute.

13 Godber, J. The History of Bedfordshire.

Chapter 2

Travellers in the Late 16th Century

A very good example of a family who were regular travellers through Dunstable was the Middletons of Wollaton Hall, Nottinghamshire. They used Dunstable as a regular overnight stop and had an arrangement for their servants to do the same. Their expenses are entered in the family papers but unfortunately, the name of the inn where the steward and servants stayed in 1573 is not recorded. Their expenditure, which included olives and capers to go with their mutton and a dessert of fruit, cheese and wine, shows that a high standard of food was available at that time. Other details show the work that such parties brought to the associated travel trades; they paid 6 shillings (30p) for fodder for the horses, 4 pence (2p) to the blacksmith for fitting a new horseshoe, and 4 pence to the saddler for repairs to their harness.

Queen Elizabeth's Travels

It has been suggested that 'Queen Elizabeth must count as the most illustrious of tourists'[14]. Even though she and her successors chose to invite themselves, as guests, to the great country houses, their progresses brought a great deal of trade. Her party which visited Theobalds in 1583 is thought to have numbered around 150 people. Woburn Abbey, which Elizabeth visited in 1572, had not yet been converted into a private house, and although Toddington manor house was newly built when she visited in 1563, neither would have been big enough to house such a large

14 Tinniswood, A. A History of Country House Visiting.

party. Perhaps the overflow stayed in Dunstable? Where the Queen went others followed, and as more and more great mansions were built, so many interested people came to view them that, by the late 1580s, a system of entrance fees and discreet tips had been introduced.

Also, so many young travellers came here from the continent that, by about the same date, phrase books and tour guides capable of speaking several languages were available in London. Having reached the capital they travelled in a circular route, taking in Cambridge and Oxford and various other new great mansion houses, including Holdenby near Northampton and Woodstock in Oxfordshire. Many of these young men must have stayed in Dunstable and used the inns, blacksmiths, wheelwrights and saddlers.

The Pilgrims

Although King Henry VIII himself visited Walsingham in 1511 and continued to send money for candles to burn at the shrine right up to Lady Day (end of March) 1538, the image of our Lady had been removed from the shrine by the time of the closure, in August of the same year.

There is no record of the shrine of St. Fremund, Dunstable during the 16th century, but that too had probably been removed before the official surrender. Nationally, although the number of travellers continued to rise, the number of people setting out on pilgrimage was already falling. However, as quoted by Colin Platt, early in the 17th century there were already those enthusiasts 'strangely thrifty of Time past' who 'goe you forty miles to see a Saints Well, or ruin'd Abbey'[15]. In other words, the tourist industry had begun.

Although it was no longer acceptable to go on a pilgrimage to Rome and other such places, each year an increasing number of people visited the continent to study architecture and broaden their education. These travellers also passed through Dunstable

---

15 Platt, C. Abbeys of Yorkshire.

and may well have stayed to study the ruins of the Priory, just as the young foreign students could have done, having crossed the Channel in the opposite direction.

The Travel Writers

For several different reasons, including royal approval and their own enthusiasm, researchers, writers and map makers began to travel around the country.

John Leland was the first well-known researcher to travel seeking information for an intended book*. He came to Dunstable just after the Priory had been closed; he noted that it had been started by Henry I and recorded some of the benefactors.

William Camden was the other important 16th century writer who came to Dunstable. He rode into the town from Hockliffe c 1571. Where the modern travellers might complain about the overpowering scent of rape, and the fact that the pollen sometimes affects the eyes of their dogs, Camden commented on the scent of the [broad] beans. He noted that it was so heavy that it confused the hounds by dulling their sense of smell! In Dunstable he noted the large pond and the Eleanor Cross which stood 'in the midest [middle] of the town'. Having written some rather confused notes about Maidenbower, he went on to relate the story of 'Dun The Robber', the founding of the royal manor house (Kingsbury) and also the Priory[16].

Camden's 'Britannia' has been reprinted several times but the first edition appeared as early as 1586.

The Map Makers

Christopher Saxton's map of Bedfordshire was published in 1579. The 1607 edition of Camden's Brittanica included an edition of Saxton's maps, prepared by William Kip.

* Due to his ill health it was never finished but his notes were published by Thomas Hearne in 1710.

16 Roucoux, O. in Topic 1985.

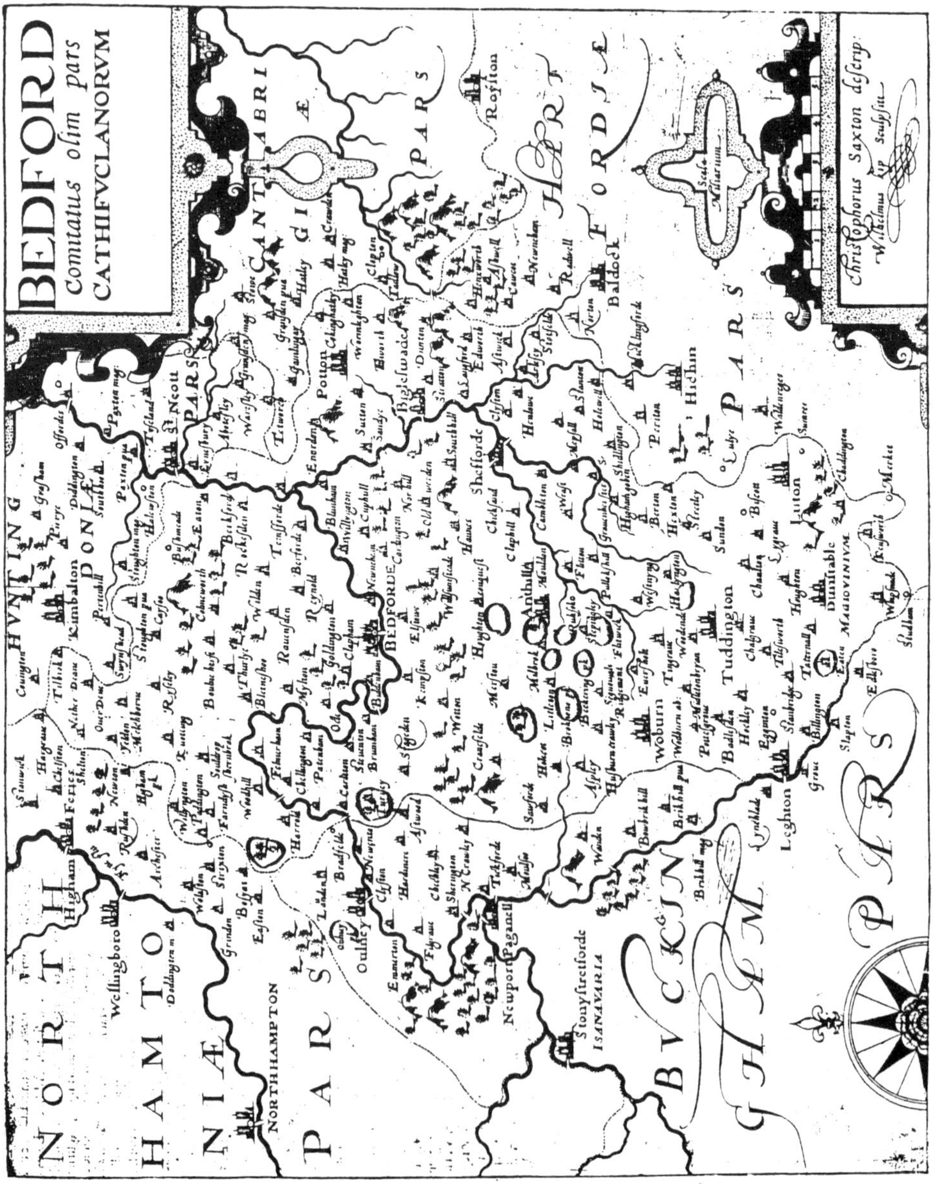

Christopher Saxton's Map of Bedfordshire prepared by William Kip in 1607.

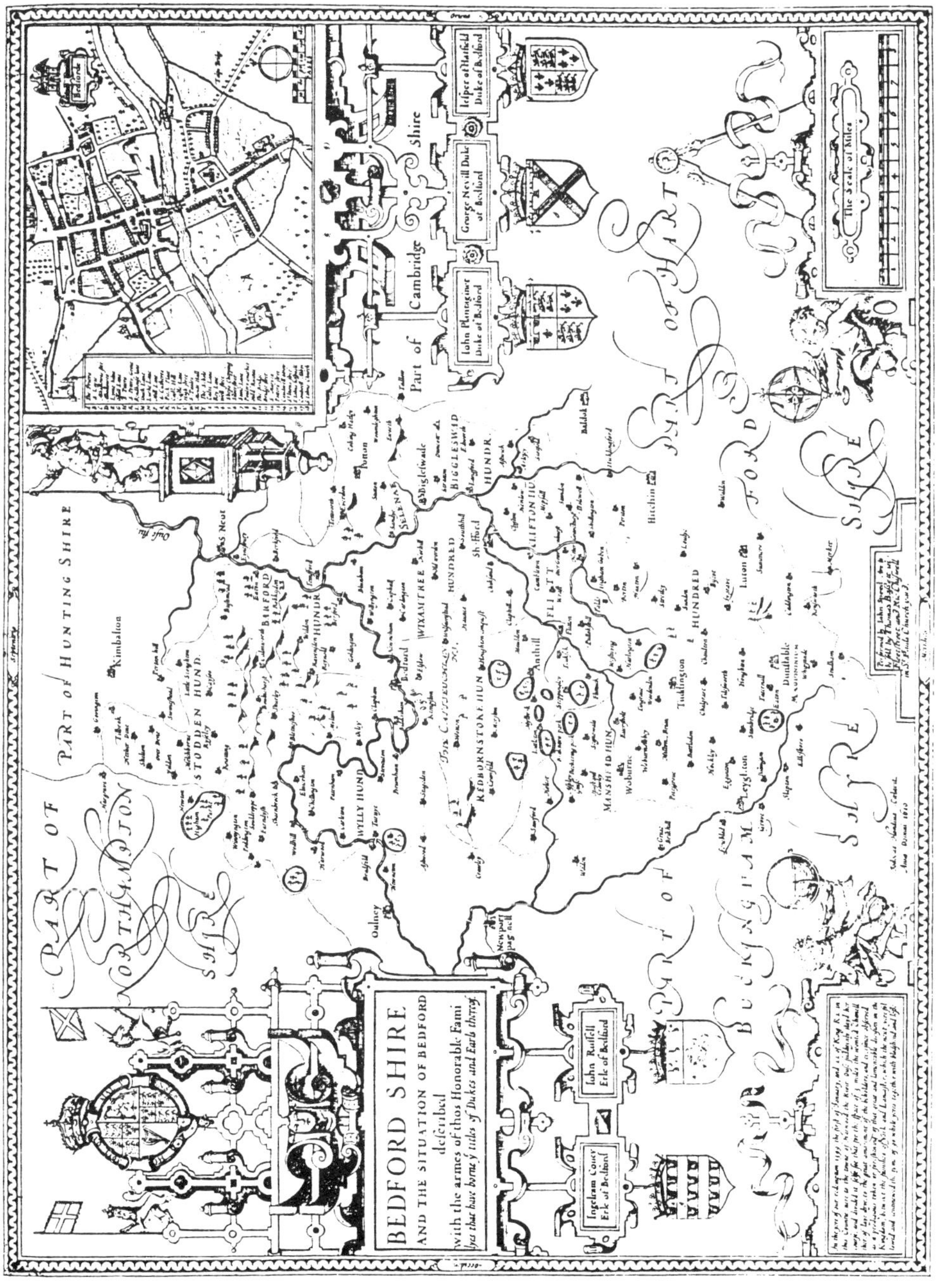

John Speed's Map of Bedfordshire published in 1610.

John Speed, who presented maps to Queen Elizabeth in 1589 and went on to publish a set of fifty maps, may never have visited Dunstable. He admitted that he had put his sickle 'to other mens corne'. In other words he gave credit to the help he had received from other people's maps. He confused the Roman names for Dunstable and Brickhill and put the name Magniovinium instead of Durocobrivis.

Both men mark Dunstable and Luton with large churches and put a low hill between them[17]. It was not until 1675 that seventy-five year old **John Ogilby** published a series of route maps based on the main roads. Dunstable is represented as a longer built-up area on the east–west road than on the north–south[18].

The Adventurers

Once again it was because of Dunstable's roadside position that the residents ran the risk of getting involved with some of the controversial political and religious matters of the day.

Sir Thomas Tresham and the Death of Queen Elizabeth

Queen Elizabeth died at Richmond Palace on March 24 1603, but her health had begun to deteriorate when she caught a heavy cold in the middle of January. A recurrence of the infection on February 28th, reduced her health and spirits even further.

For at least a year those close to the Queen and those responsible for the government of the country had been seriously concerned about the lack of a direct heir to the throne. Discussions and plans had taken place in secret for a long time, but now a decision was imperative. Elizabeth steadfastly refused to discuss the subject and for others to do so was treason. It was known that Elizabeth expected her successor to be of the direct royal line but it was not generally known that the Earl of Essex had been secretly negotiating with Elizabeth's distant young relative, King James VI of Scotland.

17 Hopkinson, M.F. Old County Maps of Bedfordshire.
18 Twaddle, W. (ed) Old Dunstable.

Even before this last infection Elizabeth had confided 'that she was a-weary of life' and now in the last weeks of her life she became increasingly depressed and found it extremely difficult to eat or sleep[19]. To the observers in and around the palace it was obvious that any day could be her last.

Scotland was a Presbyterian country which did not accept the Book of Common Prayer, whereas James's mother, Mary Queen of Scots, had grown up in France, a Roman Catholic country. Optimistically both the English Non-conformists and the Roman Catholics thought that James of Scotland was the best choice for the English throne. Nevertheless, those people who favoured James guessed, or knew, that other groups and individuals would be working equally hard in support of other candidates. When Elizabeth died it would be essential that the chosen candidate should at once be proclaimed king or queen. To be caught even preparing for a proclamation could lead to the death penalty if this was done while Elizabeth was still alive and for nearly three weeks she hung between life and death.

Various groups of people made their emergency plans; one member would stay in an anteroom at court or, depending on his social position, loiter around the stables, while another would be posted at the top of Barnet or another hill, with a good view to the south. Roman Catholic Sir Thomas Tresham of Rushton Hall, Northamptonshire, who, because of his faith, had suffered many years in prison, chose 'Luton Downs'. Ogilby, in 1675, marked this as being the top of Barton Hills but it could have been at the top of the present London Road . He had left his sons posted in and around Richmond Palace. They had arranged a signal and once it was recognised and Tresham knew that Elizabeth was dead, he would ride north as fast as he could, along what became known as the A6, until he reached Northampton.

The story starts on Thursday March 24, the day the Queen had actually died, in the early hours of the morning. Although there are varying accounts of what actually happened, it appears

---

19 Strickland, A. Queen Elizabeth.

that the news was deliberately delayed for several hours. Poor Thomas Tresham waited impatiently, convinced that his queen was dead but not daring to act until he sighted one of his sons and received the correct signal. At 5.00pm he sent one of his servants south to St. Albans and returned to his Luton inn*. Desperately he paced his room waiting for the knock which would signify the arrival of his servant or his sons. At some time in the middle of the night he became aware that the door of his room was being watched by six or eight men – probably men who did not favour James. He looked out through the shutters only to find that it was pouring with rain. Somehow he climbed out of the window, found his horse and managed to locate and pay a guide to take him into Dunstable.

He went straight to an inn, which kept horses for hire. [Possibly the Dunstable Red Lion on the corner of the cross-roads.] A semi-official letter that he carried convinced the innkeeper that he should help him. He hired two horses, one to ride and one to lead, and persuaded the innkeeper to take a chance and detain the guide until 8.00am in the morning, so that he was unable to ride back to Luton and set up the hue and cry. However, this part of the plan failed. To confuse the door-watchers, he had left his servants behind in Luton. They were quickly arrested and taken before the Lord Lieutenant, who at once sent men to chase after Tresham. They arrived too late to stop him leaving Dunstable but the innkeeper was arrested and charged with encouraging his escape.

Meanwhile Tresham rode wildly north, accompanied by two 'postboys' who would eventually take the horses back to Dunstable. As soon as it was daylight he took a chance and proclaimed that James was king to any travellers that he passed. Wanting to avoid Luton, he led the way up the Holyhead Road (A5) and only turned off for home when they reached Stony Stratford. Once his wild party of riders neared Northampton he realised it was the first day of the three day fair dedicated to the Assumption of the Virgin Mary. This would give him a

---

* Not named but possibly the Luton Red Lion.

marvellous chance to notify a great number of people at one time. They approached the town boundary between 8.00 and 9.00am, only to be caught up in a great crowd of people. Those who were approaching the fair were blocked by those who had been turned away. The mayor, knowing the general situation but not the details, had decided to postpone the fair.

The Dunstable postboys were worried about their own safety and the safety of the horses for which they were responsible and they wanted to return home. Eventually, having gained entry for himself, Tresham was obliged to let them and the horses go and walked to his house in the town. At first the mayor was far too fearful to let him proclaim King James, but later in the day the official message arrived and the proclamation was safely made[20].

Luckily it turned out that Elizabeth had died well before Tresham had reached Dunstable, and the innkeeper was released. No doubt it became one more story to be told and retold to the many travellers who broke their journey at one of Dunstable's inns.

As it turned out both the Nonconformists and the Roman Catholics were disappointed in their expectation of royal support. Thomas Tresham died on 11 September 1605 and his son Francis died in the Tower of London five weeks later. Having inherited his father's estate, Francis was drawn by his cousin, Robert Catesby, into the Gunpowder Plot.

Gunpowder, Treason and Plot

The general story of Guy Fawkes and the attempt by a group of young Roman Catholic gentlemen to blow up the Houses of Parliament, to kill King James and his sons, and to put James' young daughter, Elizabeth, on the throne, is well known. None of these young men lived in Dunstable but they must have passed through on several occasions before and after the event. A lot of the planning was carried out at Gayhurst, near Newport Pagnell. The plotters can be divided into two groups; Guy Fawkes, Percy, Catesby and his other followers, all of whom were actively involved, and those who, like Tresham, were brought in during the last few weeks.

---

20 Historical Manuscripts – Various Collections Vol. 3.

Sir Everard Digby of Gayhurst, like Tresham, was recruited for his financial help and also for his isolated house near the main road north. He was persuaded to lease a hunting lodge near Dunchurch and to organise a house party, where the conspirators could hide. Catesby's other cousins, John and Christopher Wright, and his second cousins, Robert and Thomas Winter, were, like Thomas Percy, already deeply involved but another late recruit was Ambrose Rookwood, of Coldham Hall, in Suffolk. He was probably chosen because he had an exceptionally good stable of horses.

By 1st November Rookwood had caused a stir of gossip along the Holyhead Road, by lodging teams of very high-quality horses at St. Albans, Dunstable, Towcester and Daventry. He had paid for good keep and exercise because, so he said, he expected at very short notice an invitation to join some friends at a hunting party on Dunsmore Heath.

Just before the plot was uncovered and the famous gallop north began, Francis Tresham left London for his home in Northamptonshire. Unless he branched off at Luton, he, like his father, would have ridden through Dunstable to Stony Stratford. Sir Everard Digby may have already ridden through, so that he could be at Dunchurch ready to welcome his other guests. Next to leave London were Thomas Percy, who had arranged the lease of the cellar, the leader, Robert Catesby, and Christopher Wright. Catesby's horse lost a shoe and he had to wait in Dunstable until a blacksmith could make a new one. The other two raced straight through the town to Hockliffe, where they were met by John Story, one of Percy's servants who was waiting for them with a change of horses.

The last to leave London were Ambrose Rookwood and Thomas Winter. They had been walking the streets near Westminster, waiting for Guy Fawkes to emerge from the cellar, when, unbeknown to them, a Westminster J.P. discovered Fawkes beside a great mound of coal, which hid thirty-six barrels of gunpowder! Fawkes was instantly arrested and up at street level Rookwood and Winter heard the word 'treason' and saw barriers being put up around Westminster.

Quietly, and not showing any sign of rush, they returned to their stables, mounted their horses and began to ride north. They passed out of London just as barriers were put up to close off the city. They rode as fast as possible, changing their horses at each pre-arranged stage. Winter decided to go on his own to his brother's house in Worcestershire, while Rookwood dashed on alone, making an exceptionally fast speed, possibly averaging fifteen miles per hour. Percy and Wright had left London four hours ahead of him but on the fast, well-fed horse Rookwood had picked up at Dunstable, he caught up with them on Brickhill hill.

Once the others were told of the disaster in London, they rode even faster. Shouting that they were carrying dispatches for the king, they raced through towns and villages and when their horses began to tire they even threw off their cloaks to lessen the weight. They arrived at Catesby's house at Ashby St. Ledger (near Daventry) having ridden eighty miles in seven hours. Robert Winter was waiting there for them but to their horror there were no fresh horses. So, with the minimum of rest, they rode on to Dunsmore Heath.

The story ended in disaster, with a shoot-out at their final hiding place, Holbeach House, in Worcestershire. Those few who survived the shooting, including Frances Tresham, died in the Tower[21].

The Soldiers

During earlier centuries soldiers were frequently camped in and around Dunstable and would be again in later centuries. During the latter part of the reign of Queen Elizabeth there was a threat of rebellion in Ireland. Queen Elizabeth sent soldiers under the command of the Earl of Essex and although there were many delays he eventually left London on 29 March 1599. A large crowd accompanied him for four miles out of London. No doubt many private travellers rode behind him, through Dunstable and

21 Fraser, A. The Gunpowder Plot – Terror and Faith in 1605.
Tristram, O.W. Coaching Days and Coaching Ways.
Williamson, H.R. The Gunpowder Plot.

beyond, looking for protection from his soldiers.

The weather was atrocious; there was always a shortage of supplies and the baggage wagons may well have been left behind in the mud. If so, supplies would have been bought locally, the payment being official slips of paper rather than money. If the party was short of horses or baggage wagons, the officers were empowered to commandeer them in Dunstable and leave them for collection in Little Brickhill.

In Ireland, Essex did not act as strictly as Elizabeth intended and in 1601 he was withdrawn back to England and returned down the Holyhead Road. His successor, Lord Mountjoy, made a temporary peace settlement the following year.

During the early years that James I was on the throne, there were complicated treaties and negotiations with various European countries. On 14 October 1605 a senior Irish officer wrote to the Earl of Devonshire, Lord Lieutenant of Ireland, that he had arrived in Redbourn to meet Captain William Darcy. He was expecting to meet a large party of soldiers but there were only seventy and they were camped at Dunstable. The rest were delayed by storms across the Irish sea. Captain Darcy had recruited a large troop of Irish volunteers which he intended marching right across England, to meet ships provided by the Spanish Ambassador and go to fight in the Netherlands. Because of the delay, the officers decided to leave the soldiers they had brought to England, at Dunstable, until they had received further instructions. However, eleven days later, the Earl of Devonshire's correspondence 'conceives [that] it were not unfit for [an officer to stay] with the men at Donstabill . . .'. No boats had yet been provided for embarkation and Devonshire did not want them to go any further south in case an order was eventually given for them to be transported back to Ireland[22]. They were eventually moved south but in June were stranded in Ilfracombe, where they were threatening to riot because of food shortages.

Soldiers were one of several groups of visitors who were not popular in Dunstable.

---

22 Historical Manuscripts – Various Collections Vol. 3.

The Criminals

Both markets and inns attracted all types of thieves and criminals. Just as today, the main roads made it easy for criminals to move from one town to another, e.g. in 1596 the Duke of Buccleuch, who was a Justice of the Peace in Northampton, noted that 'Robinson from Yorkshire and Kitson from Somerset two common horse stealers do use Bennell's house in Dunstable'. [The Peacock.]

If men like this were apprehended, they were taken to Bedford to wait in gaol until the sheriff held his court. Some of the records for this court are in the Bedfordshire County Record Office [BCRO] and more of these travelling criminals, or opportunists, will appear in a later chapter.

The Workforce

Having looked at two extremes of travellers, one must remember that the majority were probably honest and hard-working men and women, travelling to and fro on business or from one job to another. The conversion of the once-religious into private houses provided a great deal of work for stone masons, carpenters and other building workers, interior designers and designers of landscape and gardens.

The wealthy city businessmen, and court officials, who bought the old monastic sites, often spent money on the local churches as well as on their own new houses.

Stonemasons and Other Building Workers

Although each ex-monastic site became a place for buying ready-prepared stone, there was still a great demand for stone from the nearby Totternhoe quarry. Great loads of stone, being dragged through on slow-slung carts by oxen or heavy draught horses, must have been a daily occurrence.

In later centuries famous architects like Wyatt and Brown would have been regular visitors to the town but in the 16th century the master masons were their own architects, surveyors and contractors of labour. They were very highly respected and would have stayed at the better inns. Freemasons, who carved with and against the grain of the stone, would have very much appreciated the texture of Totternhoe stone and used it in most of the big houses in this area. Equally, local men, who had acquired their training at Totternhoe, travelled as skilled masons; their names can be found amongst those masons working at recorded building sites.

Alongside the masons were carpenters, painters, and workers in metal and glass. Specialist artists who painted murals, or who worked with stained glass, embroiderers and other who worked internally, followed the masons from site to site to quote, measure and design, before setting up their studios or returning to their own base to continue the work[23].

The Seasonal Workers

Groups of men and women crossed the county on their way to help with the harvest of various farm and garden crops. They came from many places in the west, especially Wales and Ireland, where there was high unemployment. They saved their earnings to take home for the winter and mainly camped in fields rather than using even the most humble of inns.

The Drovers

Every year thousands, maybe some years, hundred of thousands, of sheep from Wales, and fat cattle from Cheshire and Western Scotland, joined the livestock fattened on the hills of middle England and were walked down to London. By the time that they reached Hockliffe many of them were too thin for market and were kept there, and fattened, before re-starting their journeys. As far as possible they followed the green lanes and drover routes but for the time when they arrived in Dunstable and Markyate, in the parish of Kensworth, it was once possible to see the small narrow fields, alongside the road, which were probably used to graze travelling livestock overnight.

---

23 The British Museum Press has a series of books describing the work of the craftsmen.

Only one drover is named as such in the Parish Register; during the plague outbreak, of 1593, 'A strange drover from the cage' [the lock-up] was buried. Did they isolate him because they recognised the infection or did he try to drown his sorrows? No doubt some of the men put down as 'strangers', were actually drovers. Names like 'William Davys', and 'David ap Evans', sound Welsh and the burial name of 'Evence' is followed by the entry 'a Welchman'!

A Drover 'Road' passing across Dunstable Downs. (OR)

The Itinerants

Throughout the Middle Ages, and into this century, there were men and women who made a living either following five regular routes a week, a variety of day routes, or long distance routes which, throughout a long summer, took them right across the country. The cry of 'rag-a-bones', followed by the gift of a home-made paper windmill on a stick, is well remembered in Dunstable.

Only one stranger, Thomas Phillipes, who was buried in 1609, was identified as a *chapman*, but *travelling salesmen*, with a pack-pony or donkey and cart, *petty chapmen*, with their trays of small haberdashery tools, thimbles, needles and tapes, must have been very common travellers through the town. It is quite likely that on a Monday morning, queues of salesmen would have been seen, outside some merchant haberdasher, in Dunstable's High Street. 'Manchester' men and other similar titles, explained the type of cloth carried by these itinerants. Names varied in different parts of the country. *Pedlars* were probably the same as petty chapmen, whereas *tranters* worked their way across the country selling regional goods such as pottery seconds. *Higglers* would have been very well known in Dunstable as they travelled round farms, buying eggs, butter, cheese, rabbits, etc. and hawking them at the markets or at the back doors of inns.

The Entertainers

Not only the roads but also the inns and the fairs attracted many types of entertainers. Musicians, actors, dancers, small travelling theatre groups, contortionists, acrobats, dancing bears, fire-eaters and many others would all be prepared to set up their act in an inn courtyard to earn a free night's lodging.

Dunstable – A Town of Much Variety

With most residents living on, or nearly on, the four main roads, the coming and going of royal and other colourful, glamorous parties, the noise of pack-ponies with their bells, the colour, the noise, the gossip and the scandal, the entertainment and the excitement must have made Dunstable a fascinating place in which to live.

Chapter 3

Problems of Religion Facing 17th Century Dunstable

Why Dunstable?

Undoubtedly it was the importance of the roads and inns which dominated the economic history of the town, but the subject which for several periods of the 17th century influenced the social history, was religion. Yet even on this subject, the most likely reason why the small market town of Dunstable should have become a national leader in the struggle against the Established Church, was probably due to those same roads which brought interesting, and sometimes controversial, people to the inns.

Discussion in a Dunstable Inn

When Carl Philippe Moritz returned to London, after a journey south from Northampton in the 18th century, he wrote an account of his journey and included the fact that they had breakfasted in Dunstable. He had spent the night packed into a stagecoach with two tenant farmers, 'bloated with beer and brandy'. On the coach they only talked of sheep but, cheered and refreshed by a good Dunstable breakfast, their own tea, and some of Moritz's coffee, they 'regained their normal spirits . . . and began a discussion on religion and politics'. One of them . . . 'brought the story of Samson on the carpet'. His local parson had recently explained this, but he [the farmer] had all sorts of doubt about the great gates which Samson carried away and the foxes with the firebrands between their tails, although otherwise he was firm in his faith. They told each other all sorts of stories from the Bible – not as if they propounded the truth, but simply as good stories which they had heard. For the most part they had heard them from the parson and not read them personally[24].

Busy as the staff must have been, dashing to and fro with the hot and cold food, tea and coffee, one wonders if any Dunstable people overheard this conversation and reopened it later in the public bar. This conversation may have been indiscreet but it was not illegal at the time. However, we must understand that a public discussion of this nature a century earlier would have been illegal.

King James I and the Hampton Court Conference

John Richardson's first court appearance, recounted in the introduction, was ten months after the death of Queen Elizabeth. When King James I arrived in England, those worshippers who desperately wanted to break away from the Prayer Book services had pinned their hopes on his help. A group of sixteen 'Puritan Ministers of the Lincoln Diocese' met him at Hinchingbrooke House, Huntingdonshire, and presented him with a petition for the 'removal of abuses'. The following year another group handed him a similar petition when he was hunting at Theobalds in Hertfordshire. King James set up a conference at Hampton Court to listen to different shades of opinion. The group which are described as 'Puritans' wanted to reform the Church of England, but also present at the conference were 'Independents', who wanted to dispose of the whole church hierarchy. They believed that the man who led their worship should be chosen locally, not presented to them by a distant bishop. James was very shocked and refused even to discuss their demands. However, he did agree to set up a panel to translate the Bible into English and then to publish it, while strictly upholding the Established Church.

24 Quoted by – Margetson, S. Journeys by Stage.

The Rev. Edward Alport – Bigot or Victim?

The clergyman at the centre of the great Dunstable scandal was the Rev. Edward Alport. The actual date of his installation is not recorded but his name first appears in the records in 1609. The great scandal was caused because Alport, as a conforming minister, relied entirely on a service which was prayer-book-based but he was not good at preaching sermons. In many towns and villages he would have been accepted with nothing more than behind-the-scenes grumbling and, at worst, contempt. In Dunstable, because of their exposure to the free thinkers of the day such an attitude and ability was not enough. On average they were probably better-educated than most and were certainly better informed. *They wanted Bible-based services and well-thought-out sermons based on biblical teaching**.

In the villages around Dunstable, the vicars were very unsympathetic to the nonconformists or 'dissenters', as they were called. Several individuals in their congregations had been prosecuted for not attending church but the people of Dunstable had been sheltered by their minister, John Richardson. Now he had been replaced by a particularly strict conformist whose attitude to the services, along with his unsympathetic attitude to his congregation, was sure to lead to disaster.

Similar isolated events also happened in other parts of England and as they occurred more than ten years before John Bunyan was born, he must have heard of the events which took place in Dunstable, as a 'Cock and Bull' story in the inns of Elstow**.

Alport's Ordeal

A large cross-section of the parishioners of Dunstable, and Upper Houghton Regis, intended to keep worshipping in the way to

* For a more detailed explanation of this complicated situation see Godber, J. History of Bedfordshire, and Bell, P. Belief in Bedfordshire.

** Stories told at the Cock, Stony Stratford were said to be exaggerated out of recognition by the time they were recounted, at the Bull, further along the street.

which they had become accustomed – and Alport had no intention of giving way. They felt that the Priory was their church and if he would not fit in, he must move away. For some years there was armed neutrality but eventually Alport became a prisoner in his own parish; if for any reason he wished to miss Sunday services, they refused to let his locum into the church and invited an unordained 'lecturer' into the pulpit in his place. Over the years they turned away the vicars of Houghton Regis and Totternhoe as well as several others. As the disagreement between minister and congregation became more bitter, they even reported him to the church authorities for not providing a locum!

The Bizarre Baptism

In 1616, after about two years of increasing bitterness which was rapidly getting out of control, Alport took twenty-six men, four ladies 'and others yet unknowne' to the court of The Star Chamber. The proceedings started with an account of a previous court case concerning an event which took place on November 16th 1614.

'Upon or about the sixteenth daye of the moneth of November . . . 1614 did in disgrace scorne and Contempt of the sacred sacrament of Baptisme and of the preachinge and publishinge of God's most holy and blessed word and to the intent to cast scandall and disgrace . . .' upon Edward Alport and did 'move purswade incourage Countenance and abbett John Preston, Richard Saltman, Ralph Bigge and others of Dunstable aforesaid as yet unknowne . . .', did bring a sheep into the church and 'into the pulpit erected and imployed for preachinge in the same parish Church and unto the font stone there erected and imployed for ye said ministration of the Sacrament of Baptisme a sheepe'.

He then described how **they baptised the poor sheep with the name, Edward Alport.** I think we can interpret this desperate act as illustrating their belief that even a sheep could preach as good a sermon as Edward Alport! Not surprisingly, Alport had reported them to the Archbishop of Canterbury and to the highest court in the province of Canterbury. The three

The sheep is baptised and given the name Edward Alport.

'Edward Alport' preaching a sermon. I am grateful to artist Mrs Brenda Mills for the use of these two pictures.

ring-leaders were found guilty and excommunicated by the Commissioners for Ecclesiastical causes. They were also sentenced to 'public corporal punishment and penance'.

The Punishment

The word 'excommunication' has today lost its reflected terror; we have forgotten that no-one could speak to an excommunicant, not even closest members of their family, no-one could treat them if they were ill or even accompany them to their grave. As a result no-one could offer them employment – they and their families were destitute. Needless to say, they were forbidden to attend communion. In a not-too-serious case the way for an excommunicant to show public penance was to attend worship, four Sundays running, dressed in a white, sack-like gown, to confess their fault before the whole congregation, and to prostrate themselves in front of the altar throughout the service. The baptism of the sheep had caused such a widespread scandal that there had to be extreme public penance, accompanied by corporal punishment. It is possible that on each of the four Sundays they had to walk around the four roads of the town, in their white sacks, before going into church. Also, they would either have been 'solemnly scourged', i.e. whipped with thongs tipped with metal, outside the church, or beaten on their bare backs as they were dragged around the town behind carts.

That is what should have happened. How severe the scourging was we do not know but the event appears to have united the group and far from becoming destitute, or being kept out of church, their friends combined to help them. According to Alport, the offenders were:

'unlawfully mentayned abbetted incouraged Countenanced and supported by the rest of the said confederates with divers summes of money for their incouragement to persist in the same Contempt and to suppresse and Conceall the names of the said Confederates'.

As far as attendance at church was concerned, he later reported that two of the other offenders had, without being elected, taken on the role of churchwardens and smuggled at least one of the excommunicants into the communion service. So in other words, they tried to hide the names of the offenders and if they were caught, supported them and their families financially.

The Reason for the Bizarre Behaviour

It seems hard to believe, but these people were not trying to show any disrespect to God but just the reverse. They were thoughtful, enquiring, well-read people, familiar with the biblical stories and desperate to have a clergyman who would use his time in the pulpit, to explain the meaning behind these stories. 'What was the background to . . .?' 'Why did Jesus say . . .?' 'What was the connection between some Old Testament story and . . .?' Instead of this, they were probably getting a series of homilies, possibly even read out of a book. These were probably based on biblical passages which stressed the need for good behaviour, loyalty to church and king, generosity towards repairs of the church and for the care of the poor and sick in their parish.

It was because such a large part of the congregation felt so passionately about their services, their lack of biblical teaching and their inability to get a change of minister, that they were prepared to take part in the revolt; or to help those whom Alport described as the 'confederates'.

The Court at the Star Chamber

During the reign of Henry VIII an old court had been remodelled to deal with cases concerning 'riots, perjury and other misdemeanours'. It operated with a panel of lords, spiritual and temporal, plus two law judges, but *without a jury*. The full account of the Dunstable case, with explanatory notes, is published in BHRS Volume XI.

Edward Alport Complained of Violence

Having set out the sacrilegious case of the bizarre baptism, Alport then moved on to the gradual built up of their efforts to drive

him out of the town. He complained that having shut his locums out of the church, they then reported him to the church authorities for neglecting his parish but that, as months went by, the situation became more violent. The group that he referred to as the 'confederates' would have claimed that the violence was started by Alport himself, but he claimed that it was them. He insisted that Joseph Medgate and John Turvey committed perjury, when they complained to the court that he, Alport, had trespassed on Medgate's land and 'thrust a pitch forke' at Medgate's son. He swore that they had told the court a pack of lies when they complained of his quarrelsome behaviour which, they said, had continued since his arrival in Dunstable.
He complained that:

1. in October they had reported him and his wife to a Justice of the Peace, concerning a charge of assault and battery. On top of which they 'unlawfully Combined and conspired and threatened to drive . . . [Alport] out of the towne and Countrey . . .'.
2. that they threatened, that if they were not successful via the lawcourt, they would '. . . inhumanely, blouddely and Cruelly to shoote . . . [Alport] . . . and have mutually bound themselves with an oath to shoot and wound . . . [Alport] . . . with pistoll and either to kill him or make him never able to helpe himselfe'.

Drink Made Them Brave – and Foolish

He had cause to believe this threat, not because it was true but because, when the group was 'in drink', their behaviour was most threatening. On 10th August 1615 the whole group, including the four ladies, had met at an alehouse at ten o'clock at night, armed themselves with sticks, pitchforks and pistols and made a 'forcible and riotous entrie' into Alport's land, in the common field but not far from his house. They then sent a messenger to wake him and warn him that someone was about to cut and spoil his un-ripe wheat. They were hoping that he would come out to the field so that they could jeer at and frighten him. However, he stayed where he was. When he refused to come out, about twenty-seven of them fetched pails and barrels of strong ale and beer, and gathered under his bedroom window. There they:

'unlawfully, licentiosely, and dissolutely drunke and quaffed of great draughts of that stronge ale and beare . . . from 10 : of the clocke at night till one in the morninge till they had drunke 2 : or 3 : barrells of beare and then forciblie and riotousely entered into . . . [Alport's] . . . Grayne . . . then wasted and spoyled . . .' six acres of grain corn not yet ready for harvest.

The next day they procured a warrant, from a local justice, saying that Alport had broken the peace. They then waited, until they knew that he had gone to explain to the justice, and carried away the rest of his corn.

That evening Richard Knowles, Thomas Medgate, Joan Medgate and nine or ten others met at 'an alehouse neare to the townes end'*. Apparently they had met to discuss the fact that Alport had lodged a counter-charge against their claim. According to Alport, as the evening wore on they, including Thomas Medgate himself, encouraged Thomas Morgan, Medgate's servant, to 'assult beate and spoyle' Alport. He claimed that, egged on by the others, Morgan 'did with great stones beate batter and sore wound . . . [and] almost killed . . .' Alport. Morgan was subsequently taken before a justice, where, according to Alport, he affirmed that 'hee was sorry hee had not beate out . . . [Alport's] braines for then he should have bine well rewarded of Joseph Medgate his maister and the rest of his said Confederates'.

Alport claimed that, even then, they weren't satisfied; he said that Medgate, his brother, son, servant and four others, went once again into the common field, this time when Alport and his wife were working there. They forcibly drove the frightened couple away, cut the rest of their corn and carted it away. Some of Alport's servants, who tried to stop them, were dragged into the town and put in the stocks.

Once Alport's case was finished, first the four ringleaders, and then the four constables, put their cases. Those involved with the

* By this time Thomas Medgate was part owner of the Bull, not in North Street but at the further end of South Street.

baptism admitted their guilt and that they had already done their penance. Then they explained their side of Alport's other complaints[25].

Let Off With a Caution?

There is no record of the judge's decision but there is no evidence of further penance or excommunication. Nor is there any record of what happened at the Priory Church, until 1625 when the next incumbent, Zachary Symmes, arrived and there is then reference to a previous unsatisfactory incumbent.

Were They Guilty?

We shall never know exactly what happened in Dunstable during the years 1614–1616. Miss Godber interprets Alport's complaints, of being 'much maligned by insolent and refractory persons', as 'being the subject of coarse practical jokes and rough treatment'[26].

The Riots, Routs and Misdemeanours

On the one hand, the above struggle between the Dunstable clergyman and his congregation during the reign of James I appears to be a local disagreement, caused by an insensitive incumbent. On the other hand, it can be seen as a symptom of revolt, welling up under the surface, right across the country. During the reign of James' son, an increasing number of different sections of the country were sufficiently incensed to consider, if not riots, at least civil disobedience. It is not usually possible to look in detail at the protesters but here in Dunstable they are well recorded.

Who Were the Confederates?

We can trace most of them through the parish registers and several of them were of the class of tradespeople who made wills. However, it needs more family research before the comments below can be confirmed.

---

25 BHRS, Vol. XI.
26 Godber, J. History of Bedfordshire.

The four ringleaders who answered to the charges included *Robert Finch*, the merchant who made his will in 1652. He was nearly fifty and was probably a member of the wealthy family of haberdashers. Although some of these were strict Anglicans, Roger could have been influenced by followers of Martin Luther, while he was trading abroad. In his will he left his copy of Calvin's 'Institutes' to his son, Samuel, who was baptised at the Priory Church in 1604. Finch and *John Turvey* were, it was claimed, the two intruded church wardens. Turvey is a more shadowy figure as, at the time of the incident, his family do not appear in either Dunstable or Houghton Regis parish registers. However, the Medgate family are well recorded. *Joseph Medgate* was baptised in Dunstable in 1560. The family had property in Dunstable, including a share in the original Bull inn. Soon after 1606 Joseph and his son, *Thomas Medgate*, bought Calcutt Farm, at Houghton Regis. Even before the court case, they appear to have used All Saints Church at Houghton Regis for family ceremonies. Thomas junior inherited Calcutt from his father. *Joas Medgate* was his younger brother and was seventeen at the time of the court case. *Elizabeth Medgate* may have been the unmarried sister who was baptised in September 1570. *Margery Medgate* may have been Thomas's daughter, baptised in 1594. The year after the court case *Richard Knowles* married Margaret, daughter of Joseph Medgate, at All Saints church. He appears to have been a newcomer to the town, as this is the first time he appears in the records. Before leaving the Medgate family, *Thomas Morgan* is described as their servant. Referring to his statement before the justice, one wonders if he was a little simple? He was probably the Thomas who was in his late twenties and married with young children. Very little else is known about him but most of the Morgans were, for several generations, respected tradesmen and innkeepers.

The four constables, charged with misdirecting their duties, appear to be respectable middle-aged men. The best recorded is *William Osmond*. Three years after the court case, he is recorded as renting a dwelling house and tithe barn for two shillings and sixpence (12 1/2p) a year. He made his will in 1644; he described himself as yeoman and held land in Houghton Regis, Caddington and Kensworth, two tile kilns, one in Dunstable and one in Aldbury, and two cottages in Dunstable, in addition to his dwelling-house. He made a very responsible will, providing for his natural son and, when his daughter died, adding a codicil to provide extra support for his two granddaughters. *Richard Saltman* was baptised at the Priory in 1565, and in 1594 had married a widow who had lost her husband and children in the previous year's outbreak of plague. He died five years after the court case, aged fifty-six, and despite the troubles was buried at the Priory Church. *Matthew Hickson* was married to *Joan Dyne* (or Dyve); their children continued, after 1616, to be baptised at the Priory Church. He is probably the same man who donated to what became known as the Poor's Land Charity. The fourth constable was *William Buckmaster* from a family well-known in Houghton Regis but less so in Dunstable.

Most of the other people were only accused of being caught up in the various ale house riots and are not well recorded. However, it should be noted that, amongst them, there was a William Webb. The Webbs were a large Dunstable family and William may have been the young man who married, at the Priory Church, at the time of the court case. The Elizabeth Webb, who in 1605 married the Rev. John Richardson, *may* have been his elder sister.*

---

*I am grateful to Mrs Olive Bass for help with the above families.

Chapter 4

The Troubled Reign of Charles I

Charles I came to the throne in 1603 and inherited the problems which had built up during the reign of his father. One of the most explosive was still the subject of religion.

Changes Took Place at the Priory Church

The date has not been recorded when Edward Alport eventually left Dunstable but it was in 1625, the first year of the reign of King Charles I, that the Rev. Zachary Symmes arrived. The real attack against the nonconformists had not yet begun and the movement in favour of a bible-based form of service was growing. In London, a committee was formed to train young men in this style of preaching. They based their training on St. Antholin's church in London and a sympathetic committee raised money to buy rectories, or the right of presentation, in towns where they knew that this type of minister would be made welcome.

Zachary Symmes Becomes Vicar

In April 1625 they paid £350 for the 'Impropriation pertaining to the Priory Church St. Peter, Dunstable', and Zachary Symmes, who had trained at Emmanuel College, Cambridge was installed. He had been gaining experience by giving a series of early morning lectures at St. Antholin's in London. The committee, composed of four clergy, four lawyers and four businessmen, paid him £20 per year and provided an extra £20 per year to allow him to be resident in the town[27]. When Symmes arrived, he found that the chancel was in such a bad state of repair that it was necessary to pay £25 for repairs to be carried out[28].

Symmes was born on 5th April 1599, at Canterbury, where his father was an ordained vicar but tolerant of the reform movement. When he left university, Symmes was at first tutor to the children of his father's patron. It was in 1621 that he was invited to train at St. Antholin's but nearly four years passed, until he was twenty-six years old, before he moved to Dunstable. He and his wife had one young baby when they came to Dunstable and six more were born during their stay. There is no record of any complaints from the people of Dunstable, and it appears as though, for the next seven years, there was sympathy and respect between the vicar and his congregation. This was brought to an abrupt end by Archbishop Laud.

Archbishop Laud

Ross Lee, writing an analysis and description of Bedfordshire and the Civil War, points out that when Charles I began his reign, the national church had been in existence for less than seventy years, and that he was the first king of England to have been brought up in the Anglican faith[29]. In 1626, when Symmes first came to Dunstable, John Williams, Bishop of Lincoln, was more tolerant than the later bishops; William Laud was Bishop of London and both tutor and influential friend to Prince Charles. Once Charles was king, he promoted Laud to the position of Archbishop of Canterbury. The changes that he made throughout the Diocese of Lincoln are reported by Lee and by the Rev. John Brown in his study of John Bunyan and his background[30]. As far as Dunstable was concerned, while Laud was still Bishop of London he encouraged Parliament to make illegal the committee who were supporting Symmes and many other specialist lecturers. It was disbanded in 1633.

---

27 BCRO, A.D. 907. He rented the old manor hourse for £17 per year.
28 Calder, I.M. Activities of the Puritan Faction of the Church of England.
29 Lee, R. BHRS Vol. 65.
30 Brown, J. His Life, Times and Work.

Because of the law which confined people to their own parish churches, churchgoers from the villages were unable to attend Symmes' service in Dunstable. Desperate to find a source of biblical instruction, an increasing number slipped away to attend *unofficial meetings* which were held by un-named lecturers on the Kensworth side of Dunstable. Rumours of these meetings drifted back to Lincoln and Canterbury.

In August 1634 Archbishop Laud, who planned to send a team of inspectors round England, decided to start with the diocese of Lincoln. Dr John Farmery, Chancellor of the diocese, prepared some notes for Laud's officials, and warned them that in Bedfordshire and Buckinghamshire they would find that the people were particularly inclined to 'run from their own parishes after affected preachers'.

The enquiry started in Lincoln on 9th August 1634 and moved over to Bedford by the 26th. Group by group, the clergy were ordered to attend the enquiry and to report their attitude to, and their way of observing, the rules of the Established Church. From the north of the county Peter Bulkley, rector of Odell, made an excuse not to attend. He eventually reported to a hearing at Aylesbury, where he confessed that 'he never use the surplisse, or the crosse in Baptisme'. He was reported to the Archbishop's court but made the enormous decision to take his family to start a new life in New England*.

Zachary Symmes Leaves Dunstable

Several other ministers were warned or reprimanded but the report from Dunstable has not been discovered. The committee supporting Symmes having disbanded in 1633, this was the last year that he signed the parish register. By the time that Archbishop Laud's inspector left Lincoln, Symmes and his family were already on board The Griffin, heading for America! Two or three other Dunstable families travelled with them and arrived in Boston on 18th September 1634[31].

* The members of the present congregation of Odell exchange visits with the congregation of Bulkley's American church at Concorde.

31 Banks, C.E. The Topographical Dictionary of 2,885 English Emigrants.

They Were Made Very Welcome

By early December 1634 Zachariah* and his family had been admitted to the Baptist church at Charlestown and so great was his reputation that two weeks later he was 'elected and ordained teacher' (preacher)[32]. The group had been together for four years and had a second meeting place in Boston.

At this time new churches were continually springing up in different centres. From Charlestown, Symmes encouraged the setting up of a Baptist church at nearby Woburn. He preached their opening sermon on 21st November 1641.

The Symmes Family in America

Zachariah and Sarah had a very large and apparently happy family. Back in England two of their first three children had died as babies. Sarah was still a baby when they arrived in Dunstable and William was born less that a year later. Babies continued to arrive nearly every year. Hannah, born in 1632 soon died but the two eldest plus Mary (born in 1628), Elizabeth (1629), Huldah (1630) and Rebecca (1633) travelled with them. We can not imagine how dreadful the journey must have been but more children began to arrive once they were settled in Charlestown. Ruth was the first, in 1635, followed by Zachariah (1638), Timothy (1640 but died in 1641), Deborah (1642) and Timothy (1643).

This large family grew up and married within the church. Several of them and their children were mentioned in Zachariah's will. His salary was partly in the form of land and the family lived with modest comfort. In his will Zachariah made an intriguing reference to his brother William – he knew that his wife Sarah would join with him in making a small gift in 'remembrance of the very great love and costs to us and ours'[33].

The first son, who died, may have been baptised Zachariah,

---

* Written records from America refer to him as Zachariah.

32 Hill, H.A. The History of The Second Boston Church, Boston.

33 I am grateful to Mr John Lunn for bringing to my attention 'A Biographical Sketch of The Rev. Zachariah Symmes' which was privately published in Boston, 1873, by John Adams Vinton.

after his father, but the William, whose name appears in the Dunstable parish register, must have been named after this uncle. It may be that when the family realised that the committee who employed Zachariah were at risk and that the rectory of Dunstable would soon return to the Crown, William found the money for the passages to America. It is just possible that he remained in England and became one of the above-mentioned panel of lecturers.

Another item mentioned in the will is a 'library' valued at £15*. His skills as a teacher and preacher were greatly respected and quite early on Symmes had been made an official of the new colony. After his death, which was on 4th February 1670, a memorial stone was erected which records that:

'A prophet lies under the stone:
His words shall live tho' he be gone'[34].

It is no wonder that the congregation at the Priory Church of St. Peter in Dunstable, worshipped so peacefully during the ministry of this educated and respected minister.

Other Dunstablians Went to America

On at least two occasions in the last fifteen years descendants of the Symmes family have visited the Priory Church and the author has received letters from the descendants of other emigrants who travelled out at the same time as the Symmes family. Fran Eager of Concord USA, tells me that she is descended from Robert Long who sailed to Charlestown, on The Defence, in July 1635. He was listed as 'inn holder' but does not appear on the rent list of 1624 which probably indicates that his inn was privately owned and not a tenancy. After his arrival in Charlestown he was able to purchase the 'Great House' for £30. Zachary, son of Robert Longe, was baptised in Dunstable in 1630. His mother, Sarah, died at his birth and it was step-mother, Elizabeth, who sailed to America.

Zachary, son of Thomas Line, (Lyne) was baptised at the

* The rest of his household (furniture) was only valued at £21.

34 Vinton, J.A. (see 33).

Priory Church in 1631. It may be a complete coincidence but Thomas Lynde of Dunstable actually sailed out in the same ship as the Symmes family. His descendent, Joan Main, lives in England. Bank's dictionary of emigrants also lists Richard Haines, William Haynes and Thomas Buckmaster as travelling to Massachusetts at about the same time.

Dunstable Massachusetts

There are several places around the world with the name Dunstable but the one known to have direct connections with Bedfordshire lies in a rural area not far from Boston. A very strong tradition connects the name of Mary Seare from Dunstable, England and her husband the Hon. Edward Tyng with the founding of this settlement.

The date of their outward voyage is unknown but the Seares were a well-known Dunstable family. On 10th May 1643 a group of businessmen from around Massachusetts Bay held a meeting in Boston. A William Tynge was appointed to confer with them; out of this meeting grew the united Colonies of New England[35]. William may not be directly connected with the Hon. Edward but the first birth mentioned in the town records was the birth of Edward's grandson – William.

Before the founding of Dunstable Massachusetts, a very large area of land, which would eventually include this and other settlements, was known as 'Brattles Farm'. A Boston merchant and soldier, Major Thomas Brattle, married Elizabeth, daughter of William Tynge during the 1640s.

A list of local gentlemen/farmers who petitioned the Governor of Boston in 1673 started with the name Thomas Brattle, followed by Jonathan Tyng and ending with the name Zachariah Long. In the middle of this list was Peter Bulkley of Concord. The purpose of the petition was to ask the governor to grant them a carefully defined, very large area of land so that they could form a new territory, based on the 'town' of Dunstable.

---

35 Calder, I.M. The New Haven Colony.

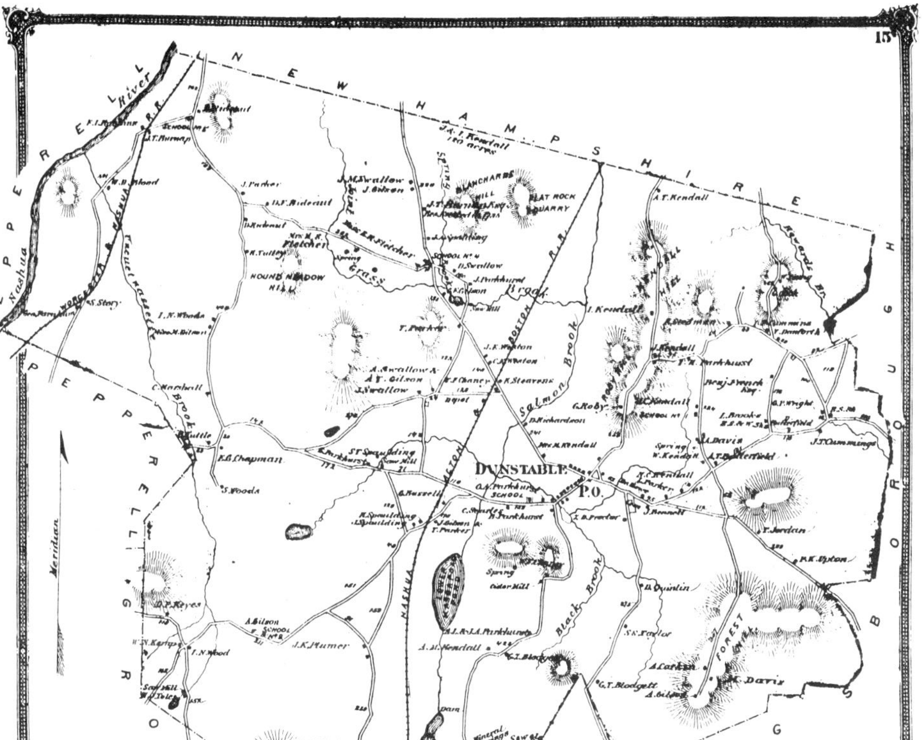

The 1875 maps of Dunstable Massachusetts from the book 'Dunstable Village' edited by Curtis S. Gates.

The role that Edward, Jonathan and their descendants played in the history of Dunstable Massachusetts is included in *A History of the Town of Dunstable* by the Rev. Elias Nason. Much of our knowledge of the history of that town and its connection with Dunstable, Bedfordshire is due to the friendship of local historian Mrs Lucy Kennedy of Dunstable Massachusetts and Mrs Pat Reeves, a member of Dunstable and District Local History Society and former Mayoress of Dunstable, Bedfordshire. As a result of this friendship there have been several visits in each direction.

The Church at Kensworth.

The minister who replaced Symmes in Dunstable was the Rev. William Pedder. To get the living at that date he must have been a strictly conforming minister, but as there are no recorded complaints from the congregation, many of them may already have been slipping away to join the dissenters at Kensworth.

Even before the visitation ordered by Archbishop Laud, the Rev. John Sydall of St. Mary's Kensworth, appears to have been confused by the large group from his congregation who were desperately seeking a Bible-based form of service, without ceremony or ritual. He refused to give in and increasingly they joined the secret meetings which were probably held on the less public part of the Downs.

Who Were the Lecturers Who Preached on the Downs?

In several parts of Bedfordshire and Hertfordshire there were landowners, sympathetic to the needs of their tenants, who wanted good teaching sermons so that they could learn more about the Bible. On one side of Kensworth, Lady Ann Bacon, at Gorhambury, St. Albans, provided a lecturer at Redbourne. On the other side, at Hemel Hempstead, the lord of the manor left money to provide a lecturer for his tenants. Despite the protests of the vicar, the parishioners chose Phillip Goodwin to preach at the Thursday morning market and on Sunday afternoons. Either or both of these could, at different times, have been the local preacher.

Although very few of the great land owners were supporters of the Independent movement many of them were anxious to reform the church. Locally, they could not see anything but good coming from a teaching sermon, whether it was preached by an ordained minister or by a so-called lecturer. By the time that the war ended, the activities of these lecturers was quite legal and until 1660 they moved freely about the country.

Once the Civil War broke out, Parliament took control of Bedfordshire and Hertfordshire. The Rev. Pedder rode away, presumably to become a royalist chaplain, leaving the Priory without a vicar. A Parliamentary committee provided a team of lecturers to preach in Dunstable and elsewhere. At both Hemel Hempstead and Kensworth the congregations managed to replace their unpopular vicars.

An ordained priest called Edward Harrison, installed at Kensworth, proved to be sympathetic to his congregation and even went with them to find out what was the attraction of the un-ordained lecturers. He was very impressed with their preaching and with their argument that church ministers should be chosen by a local committee, not by a disinterested bishop living and working many counties away. So impressed, that he officially resigned the living, moved out of the vicarage and into a cottage he had bought in the village. From there he continued to minister to the congregation until some months later, when he rode away to become secretary and confidential messenger to the local Parliamentary leader, soon to be based at Newport Pagnell[36].

During the Civil War there was a gradual change until, by the end, the whole subject of ritual presentation, form of service and choice of minister had been reversed. When the name of the local preachers were noted, many years later, a Thomas Hayward from Kensworth was prominent amongst them.

36 Whitley, W.T. Baptist Quarterly VII, No. 5, Jan. 1935.

The Threat of War Comes Even Closer

Religion was just one of many causes which forced the people of England to divide and take up arms. The judges resented the fact that monied people could buy their way free from punishment meted out by the courts. Families, who for centuries held inherited titles which were originally won on the battlefield or given for exceptional loyalty to the crown, resented the sale of titles. The landed gentry resented changes to customs which had been established even before the Norman Conquest. The big businessmen, who may have included some of the residents of Dunstable, resented export/import taxes which had been imposed without the approval of Parliament, and everyone resented the Ship Tax!

An Unpopular Tax Unites Many Worried People

Twenty years after the previous riot there was, once again, trouble in Dunstable. A cross-section of the community was involved but as it concerned taxes, more members of the business community were included. This time there was no recorded violence, just a firm refusal to pay an unpopular tax.

King Charles came to the throne in 1625 and within a few years several different sections of the population were offended by his policies. For centuries the taxes had been decided following discussions between king and Parliament. However, as bitterness and resentment grew around the country, Charles tried to force through his tax arrangements without the agreement of Parliament. Eventually his judges, including Sir Francis Crawley, whose brother many years later would buy Priory House, advised the use of a *Ship Tax*. This hadn't been used for centuries and was quite inappropriate. In 1635 Bedfordshire was assessed to pay £3,000 and managed to raise £2,900 and, with difficulty, did nearly as well in the following year. From then on it became increasingly difficult to persuade people to pay. In 1637, at which time Dunstable was assessed to pay £20.8s.0d, there was a countryside revolt, with a great number of people refusing to pay. Bedfordshire was one of the most resistant counties, with

600 people in arrears. In relation to population numbers, Dunstable was the focal point for this resistance. Fifty families were named, plus several more in Upper Houghton Regis.

It is not possible at the moment to tie up this list of names with the earlier list, but several of the families are again represented – including Roger Finch (senior and junior) and William Osmond. A change of tax collectors still failed to bring in the money and despite the harsh treatment, many remained firm and did not pay. Most of the debts were from one to five shillings but two assessments in Upper Houghton were as low as 6d (2 1/2p) and 4d. On the other hand, innkeepers Richard Briggs and John Plott (Platt) owed 16 shillings (80p) and £1.10s.0d respectively.

The Last Straw

In 1640 Charles sent for the members of Parliament to come to London, but in three weeks sent them home again. A few months later he recalled them but it was too late to discuss a peaceful settlement. Following an incident when armed soldiers had attempted to arrest members while they were sitting in the House, both sides prepared for war*.

Dunstable During the Civil War

On 29th August 1642 Charles I raised his banner at Nottingham and war could no longer be prevented. Although the people of Bedfordshire were mainly supporters of Parliament, towns, villages and even some families had divided loyalties.

Mr Michael Grigg, who is included in a quit rent list of 1619 as owning a house in Dunstable which was let out to Robert Haddon, was the town's only recorded, active Royalist[37]. He must surely be the 'Mr Grigg', on the same list, who owned the new inn, suitably called The Crowne[38]. A group of Parliamentary

* For details of the preparations and for the war itself, as it affected Bedfordshire, see Evans, V. John Bunyan, His Life and Times, and its reference section.

37 Ross, L. BHRS Vol. 65.

38 BCRO, FAC. 7.

officers reported from Bedfordshire, 28th September 1648, a list of Royalists whose estates had been sequestered on behalf of Parliament – Michael Grigg was on the list, owning property with a rental value of £111 per annum. It is of interest that one of his tenants was a 'Mr Peddar'; he *may* be the minister from the Priory who had left his living to become a Royalist chaplain. The committee for compounding (i.e. collecting) the rents of sequestered property often had difficulty collecting the money. When he owed them £1,060 in 1646, Grigg is described as of Hadley, Middlesex and of Dunstable, Bedfordshire. They were still trying to collect their money, plus interest, in July 1649. However on 28th September he was discharged[39].

A Garrison at Newport Pagnell

Soon after the outbreak of war a small garrison was set up at Bedford to defend the county. However Royalist Sir Lewis Dyve, of Bromham and Sewell, had a larger stronghold at nearby Newport Pagnell. After Dyve made an attack on Bedford in October 1643, it was decided that to defend Bedfordshire, Newport Pagnell must be taken and converted into a major Parliamentary stronghold.

The Earl of Essex was at St. Albans during these discussions and sent a large detachment of soldiers ahead to Dunstable. The Parliamentary newspaper, 'A Perfect Diurnall', reported '. . . that they had most cruelly plundered Bedfordshire in divers places, and that day past came to Dunstable . . . where was a great Faire kept that day, and made great spoile there'. Another paper blamed the people of Dunstable for inviting soldiers into the town. No October fairs are recorded for Dunstable at that time, but it may have been an end of harvest hiring fair.

These soldiers, together with reinforcements sent from London, marched on to Newport Pagnell. They were so successful that during the night of 26th October, Dyve and his soldiers marched out of the garrison without waiting to defend the site. Soon afterwards Sir Samuel Luke, of Wood End, Cople, became governor of the garrison. His notebooks have been

39 Lee, R. BHRS Vol. 65. VCH, Beds. Vol. 2.

published as BHRS Volume 42, and from these letters we can see that Dunstable was the place where army supplies, money and probably recruits and pressed men, were handed over by the escorts who had brought them from the south. Detachments from Newport Pagnell then took charge and escorted them further north. Market-stall holders and shopkeepers must have been used to food being compulsorily purchased when one or other party arrived without supplies.

An Attack on the Priory Church of St. Peter

Apart from contributing towards the cost of the Parliamentary army, the people of Dunstable had to help support the Newport Pagnell garrison; with money, food and other supplies as well as taking part in a rota, which involved supplying horses, carts and labourers. In addition, during the winter when there was usually a lull in the fighting, Parliamentary soldiers were sent into the county to be supported by the local people. The main Royalist garrison, used by King Charles and his family, was at Oxford. Being on a main road out of Oxford, Dunstable and district were, on several occasions, raided by parties of Royalist cavalry, also looking for supplies of food and more horses. One of the best reported incidents appeared in the Parliamentary news sheet, dated Monday 24th June 1644[40]. Information had been received that the Royalist forces were continually raiding Bedfordshire, Buckinghamshire and Hertfordshire '. . . committing many great and cruell outrages . . .'. On the previous Sunday, the king had passed through Hockley in the Hole (Hockliffe) on the way to Bedford and his soldiers had

'. . . plundered Leighton, and sent another party to Dunstable, where they entered the Towne when the people were at church, not contenting themselves with plunder, but made a great disturbance, cutting and slashing the people in the [Priory] Church, and shot a case of pistols at the Minister in the Pulpit, but missed him; and afterwards abused him very inhumanely'.

If it were not for the door, which still stands at the back of the church peppered with holes from the pistol shot, this might

40 A Perfect Diurnall. Number 48.

(377) Numb. 48 379

A Perfect Diurnall
OF SOME
PASSAGES
IN
PARLIAMENT:
And from other parts of this Kingdom.

From Munday the 24. of *June*, till Munday the 1. of *July*. 1644.

Collected for the satisfaction of such as desire to be truly informed.

Printed for *Francis Coles* and *Lawrence Blaikelock*; And are to be sold at their Shops in the *Old-Baily*, and at *Temple-Bar*.

Munday the 24. of June.

THis morning information was given to the Parliament, that the Kings forces, since their returne to *Oxford* according to their old trade of plundering, (the grand support of that Army) about. 6000 of them divided into severall parts, had made incursions into Bedford, Buckingham and Hartfordshire, committing many great and cruell outrages; as if His Majesty, in pursuance of all His Protestations, Proclamations, and Declarations to maintaine the Protestant Religion and liberties of the Subject, had destined the whole Kingdome to ruine that take not part with his good Catholique subjects the Irish Rebels. On the Lords day last the King passed thorough Hockley in the hole towards Bedford, and in the way plundered Leighton, and sent another party to Dunstable, where they entered the Towne when the people were at Church, not contenting themselves with plunder, but made a great disturbance, cutting and slashing the people in the Church, and shot a case of Pistols at the Minister in the Pulpit, but missed him; and afterwards abused him very inhumanely. The like outrage they committed at divers Townes and Villages thereabouts, and at Woodborne the Earle of Bedfords house. They also faced Newport Pannell, but sir *Samuel Luke* let fly 2 or 3 of his great peeces which set them packing.

The last certaine newes from the siege of Yorke. From the Lord Generall in the West; And from Sir *Wil. Waller*, and the Kings Army.

But there will no doubt be a sudden course taken to free the associated Countries of these plunderers. Essex, Hartford, Buckingham and the rest of the association

B are

A page from the Perfect Diurnal reporting the attack on the Priory Church. Facsimile from the Burney Collection in the British Museum.

Part of the door of the Priory Church showing bullet holes. No longer needed, it stands in the porch. (OR)

appear to be Parliamentary exaggeration. It was also during that visit that the Royalist soldiers visited the Red Lion (previously known as the White Swan). They knew that, in addition to his business as innkeeper, Mr Plott [Platt] the proprietor owned a flourishing stable of horses for hire. By June 1644, most of his horses must have been bought by the army or stolen by previous raiding parties. It is said that he came out of the inn to try to protect his remaining horses, only to be shot dead by the raiders[41]. Although the burial of Mr Platt's servant was registered, 24th February 1644, by June the register was no longer being used, so the later burial was not recorded.

The Eleanor Cross is Taken Down

Charles I, Prince Rupert and their senior officers must have passed through Dunstable, both following victories and defeat. After the battle of Naseby (Northamptonshire) in June 1645, the

41 Elstow Moot Hall Leaflet [EMH] Tibbutt, H.G. Bedfordshire and the First Civil War.

defeated king and the remains of his cavalry made a roundabout route back to Oxford via Stamford, Huntingdon, Bedford and Woburn, where he spent the night of 26th August. He left the abbey the following morning, and rode on to Dunstable, arriving at 2pm and rested at the Red Lion before continuing his journey to Oxford[42]. Although his soldiers returned to plunder Luton the following day, the visit to Dunstable on the 27th was probably his last visit as a free man.

The surviving Eleanor Cross, near Northampton; it was carved and decorated by the same artists as that at Dunstable. (LPE)

42 Tibbut, H.G. Op. Cit.

The statue made in 1985 by Miss Dora Barret to mark the opening of the Eleanor Cross Shopping Precinct which was developed by builders Robinson and White. (LPE)

Parliamentary officers also passed to and fro through the town. On 25th July 1643, 'John Plant ye servant of the Earl of Essex' was buried at the Priory Church. This may have been the occasion when the dispirited army were returning from defeat at Roundway Down, near Oxford. It may also be the occasion when, incensed by the crosses and other carvings that they interpreted as religious superstition, they took down the Eleanor Cross which was standing in the centre of the cross-roads. This act of violence must have come as a shock to the people of Dunstable – one of many during these difficult years.

The Death of Charles I

The troubled reign of Charles I came to an abrupt end on Tuesday 30th January 1649 with his execution outside the Banqueting House at Whitehall. During his short speech, it became clear that he had no regrets concerning his autocratic behaviour. 'a subject and sovereign' he said 'are clean different things . . .'. Yet as Antonia Fraser has said – 'For whatsoever could be said of the execution of King Charles I, that it was inevitable, even that it was necessary, it could never be said that it was right'[43].

So although there were no major battles in or around Dunstable during the years of the Civil War, and again when scattered bouts of fighting occurred in 1648, Dunstable was still a very difficult place in which to live. Right across Bedfordshire, farmers struggled to grow crops even though they were dreadfully short of labour, horses, carts and fodder, but around Dunstable the unripe crops were ruined by traffic which took short cuts across their fields. If the crops were harvested and safely in barns before they were stolen, they were commandeered by the soldiers at the lowest possible price. So food was short, prices high and little local produce was available to sell in the market or to the inns. Not only were the young men automatically conscripted when they were sixteen, but any active

43 Fraser, A. Cromwell, Our Chief of Men.

man seen when officers were scavenging for food and horses would be taken back to the nearest camp and pressed into military service.

Replica of a Cromwellian Coach as used in the mid 1650s. From the Mossman Collection. (LPE) (Courtesy of Luton Borough Council.)

Chapter 5

The Civil War's Legacy on Religion

Religious Problems Cause Many Changes

It wasn't only business, family and social life which was disrupted during the Civil War – many of the churches were also affected. In the case of Dunstable the congregation at the Priory Church of St. Peter had already experienced a series of major changes and disturbances. Back in March 1641 a very long procession had travelled south from Bedford and had probably passed through Dunstable and St. Albans, gaining size as it headed for London. Eventually about two thousand people, led by the High Sheriff, witnessed a petition from Bedfordshire being handed in to the House of Commons. In it, they thanked Parliament for removing the 'superstitious innovations' (of Archbishop Laud), the removal of illegal taxes (the Ship Tax), the abolition of the Star Chamber (where Edward Alport had summoned the people of Dunstable) and the Court of High Commission, which had been responsible for driving out Zachary Symmes. The petition then went on to ask for the removal of all evil councillors and the 'complete removal of all burdensome and scandalous ceremonies and of all corrupt and scandalous ministers'. They wanted Parliament to provide and maintain 'learned, pious, and conscientious . . . ministers . . . especially in market towns and populous places'. They didn't know it, but, in less than two years that is exactly what would happen!

As the Puritan influence in Parliament became stronger, altar rails, stained-glass windows and statues were removed and special surplices and ceremonies were forbidden. This was not because the Puritans, who were trying to reform the Church of England, were sacrilegious but because they felt that such things were both unnecessary and a distraction to the congregation.

In 1643 an Act was passed whereby clergy would no longer be ordained by a bishop but would in future be appointed by a committee, and in 1645 it became illegal to use the Book of Common Prayer, which was replaced by a 'Directory of Public Worship'.

Changes at the Priory Church of St. Peter

When the parish church was 'owned' by the Augustinian canons, they were in the position of rector, held any land which had been donated for the support of the church, collected the tithes and appointed the vicar who took the services. After the Dissolution, ownership of the church land and tithes plus the advowson (the right to appoint a vicar) passed to The Crown. Over the centuries different people bought or rented these rights. Sometimes an ordained man would hold the position of rector and take the services himself but at other times a layperson might hold the rectorial position and appoint a vicar to take the services.

Much work still needs to be done before the status of the various Dunstable clergy can be accurately decided. Where possible the following information has been drawn from diocesan records and signatures in the parish registers.

Edward Alport signed the register as 'vicar', and the corn which he tried to protect from the 'confederates' was probably growing on the glebeland originally provided by the Priory to help support a vicar. In 1625 the London Committee bought the living, presumably from the Crown, for £350 and paid Zachary Symmes £20 per year plus the 'profits of the living'. At that time the revenue of the Rectory did not exceed £40 per year and there was no vicarage. As rector they paid extra for him to live in the parish and a further payment of £25 to repair the chancel[44].

---

44 Calder, I.M. The Activities of the Puritan Faction.

The Rev. William Pedder Comes – and Goes

Before they could appoint Symmes they had to remove an 'unsuitable incumbent'. Edward Alport's last signature in the parish register is is 1619 and the registers for 1620–22 are signed only by the church wardens. In 1623 and in 1624 they are signed by William Pedder – curate. Symmes signed for the last time in 1633 and in 1634 it was William Pedder who once again sent off the transcript of the register to the bishop. He then signed the register (as Minister) from 1635–1643*.

He had daughters baptised at the Priory Church in 1635 and 1638 but we do not know if he lived in the house vacated by Symmes, or elsewhere. A further mystery is exactly when he finally left the parish. It has always been said that he departed in 1642 which is the year that a statement was made in the House of Lords that 'divers ministers in several counties have left their charges and are gone into the King's army . . .'. The statement continued with permission being given for the profits of these deserted livings to be sequestered**. However, as Pedder did not hold the church land he does not appear amongst the list of sequestered.

The panel of 'Lecturers' was set up in September 1642 but they may well have been visiting preachers and Pedder *could* have remained in the parish until 1643. This agrees with the date given by George Briggs, in his case concerning tithes[45]. He stated that Pedder 'presented himself' to the rectory of Dunstable.

Who Was William Pedder?

There is no evidence that the William Pedder, *curate* before the installation of Zachary Symmes, was other than the same William Pedder, *minister* after Symmes left for America. Pedder is a very well-known local name; in 1671, one William had a house with 3 hearths in Eaton Bray and another with 4 hearths at Streatley. There were at least six more families in other villages around Dunstable[46]. However, as we know that there was no vicarage

---

* No signatures have been found for 1636 and 1641.

** Taken for the use of Parliament.

45 BCRO, ABCP 46.

46 BHRS, Vol. 16.

provided in Dunstable, the minister's family home may have been the one entered in Luton as 'Widow Pedder', with 7 hearths. Also the Luton lists, for Ship Tax arrears in both 1637 and 1638, included a William Pedder Clerk, so they were probably a Luton family[47].

A Team of Lecturers for Dunstable

When, as in Pedder's case, the incumbent left his living it was normally filled by an individual appointed by a committee set up for that purpose. They were allowed the normal income from the living – minus a fifth which was given to the family of the sequestered minister. If the living was extremely low, it was boosted by money raised from sequestered rectorial tithes. For example, Sir Robert Napier, of Luton Hoo, had in the past received £480 each year from tithes collected in different parts of Luton. In 1644 these were sequestered and some of the money was used to increase stipends in different parts of Bedfordshire.

However, a lot of the money raised in this way was also used to support teams of lecturers. These were educated men and probably inspired preachers but they were not necessarily ordained. They were employed to run various administrative committees in London and to preach in those churches where the approved minister was unable to preach. In the case of Dunstable they were to be available, when required, to take the services in the Priory Church. It may be that at first Pedder was left to run the parish and that lecturers were only expected to preach, but at a later date they must have been solely responsible. The full list of the seventeen men available to preach in Dunstable was announced 2nd September 1642[48]. The unpublished thesis of the Rev. Conrad Hamlyn* has been deposited in the Bedford record Office with some notes concerning their later livings. However, he does not seem to have noticed that the name Symmes was included. This may well have been the William 'Simes' who in

47 BHRS, Vol. 18.

48 Shaw, W.A. A History of the English Church During the Civil War.

* The Rev. Conrad Hamlyn (d. 1973) spent several years of his semi-retirement in Bedfordshire.

1642 was installed in Meppershall rectory when the Royalist Dr Timothy Archer, lost his living[49]. Zachary Symmes had had a son baptised William, 10th January 1626, but he would only have been sixteen at the time.

The Need for a Resident Minister

There is no doubt that the lecturers were very capable men. Several of them had degrees from Oxford or Cambridge and most of them eventually settled down in good livings or, until the Restoration, had successful careers in administration.

However stimulating their services were on Sundays, as time went by the people of Dunstable began to long for a resident minister. In 1656 they sent a petition to Oliver Cromwell, which included the information that the living had 'been void this fourteen years' and that it was only worth £35, including the glebe land and the small tithes[50]. After much deliberation a small increase was made and the Rev. Isaac Bringhurst appointed. He was a graduate of Jesus College, Cambridge and had been called to the ministry in 1647. Accurate records are short at this time; he may have arrived as early as 1656 in the position of curate and then, at a later date, have acquired the rectory. If so he would then have been entitled to the great tithes*. This caused trouble with some of the residents and led to a court case.

The opportunity to become ordained would not have been available in 1647, when Bringhurst left university and it is probable that he arrived in Dunstable as an unordained curate. At some stage he probably obtained ordination and may then have bought or rented the rectory from the Crown. Whatever his position had been in the past, in 1663 he challenged George Briggs in the Archdeacon's court concerning the collection of the great tithes. These not only included cereals and fleeces but also 'enclosed grasse grounde or pasture grounde . . . [whether] growing or renewinge . . . or if [the ground] is soe eaten upp'.

---

49 Chambers, V.H. Old Meppershall A Parish History.

50 Callendar State Papers Domestic, 1656 – quoted by Conrad Hamlyn.

* The small tithes were such commodities as milk, eggs and chickens.
The great tithes were very valuable, being corn, livestock, meat, wool, etc.

Briggs, who owned The Sugar Loaf and six other inns and beerhouses, must have needed many enclosed pastures as well as straw and food for stabled horses.

He agreed that '. . . by the ancient and laudable customes of the parish of Dunstable . . . the lawful Rectors or Rectory had and have the right of tythes . . .'. He admitted that he did pay tithes when Bringhurst first arrived but that was not to Bringhurst as rector or as the lawful incumbent 'but to avoid trouble and [a lawsuit] it being in this late unhappy times of war'[51].

Having trained during the years that Cromwell was in charge of the country and having been appointed by the committee who deliberately selected men who favoured the nonconformist service, Bringhurst was probably welcomed in Dunstable by the Independents in his congregation. However, it is possible that some of the wealthier members continued to make things difficult for him. It seems likely that Oliver Cromwell himself saw the petition of 1656 and may even have been instrumental in selecting, or approving, Bringhurst's appointment.

Difficulties for Clergymen After the Restoration

The changes which had resulted in an entirely new form of church service and method of selecting and appointing clergy had taken place quite slowly. Even before the restoration of the monarchy and certainly before the crowning of Charles II, the High Church party had taken control and the prayer book service was re-introduced and strictly enforced. It was a very difficult time for clergy who had been appointed to their livings during the period when Parliament was supporting a form of service which did not use the Book of Common Prayer. As Bringhurst's two children, born in 1658 and 1659, were registered as 'born' not as 'baptised' he *may* have had Baptist sympathies. The living at Kensworth became vacant in 1660 when the Independent James Baileman was evicted, and Bringhurst moved there as vicar. However, 'moved' may not be the correct interpretation; it was quite common at that period for a clergyman to be connected

51 BCRO, ABCP 45/46. I am grateful to Mrs Joan Schneider for translating part of this long document.

with more than one living. On 6th January 1660 a London committee ordered the person who held the church land of Kensworth to add £70 per year to the £30 which Baileman was receiving. If this continued after the Restoration £100 per year was a very good salary[52]. Only the church wardens had signed the registers in 1656 and 1657 but Bringhurst signed as 'minister' in 1658 and 1659. The registers were still not being kept on a regular basis and nothing has been found for 1660 and 1661. A man with the unusual christian name of 'Bishop' Lyster signed as minister in 1662. He had been licensed as curate on 21st February 1661. This may be because Bringhurst had moved or it may have been a temporary measure until he was able to arrange the transfer of the rectory and valuable tithes.

He was officially installed on 4th April 1662 and signed the registers until 1679, even though he took on the position of vicar of Kensworth when the living was vacated by Bringhurst. The house used by Zachary Symmes had been a tenancy and part of the reason that Dunstable clergy chose to hold the two livings may have been the lack of a suitable house in Dunstable.

The next Dunstable incumbent was William Bedford MA. He signed the register as minister in 1680 but following his installation on 10th May 1681, he signed as 'rector'. However, by the end of 1682 he had become ill or decided to retire and John Lord MA was installed on 11th February 1683. Bedford was buried at the Priory on 7th August. More about the Rev. John Lord will be included in the next book in this series*.

Even the Parish Registers were Changed

It may be because of the absence of a resident incumbent, aggravated by the disruption of normal life during the Civil War, that parts of the Dunstable register are very muddled. In 1653 an

52 Urwick, W. Nonconfirmity in Hertfordshire. I am grateful to Mrs Irene Millest for pointing out this reference.

* Much research is still needed to sort out the overlappping livings of Dunstable, Kensworth and Toddington. Also the roles played by John Lord senior and his son, also called John.

order came from Parliament that in each parish the people should appoint a secular *Register* (registrar). Their choice was to be approved by a local magistrate and from then on the person chosen was responsible for recording all the births and deaths as they occurred*. He also had to record the reading of the banns of marriage – *wherever this took place*; in Dunstable this was in the market place. The actual marriage was to take place before a magistrate, not a clergyman.

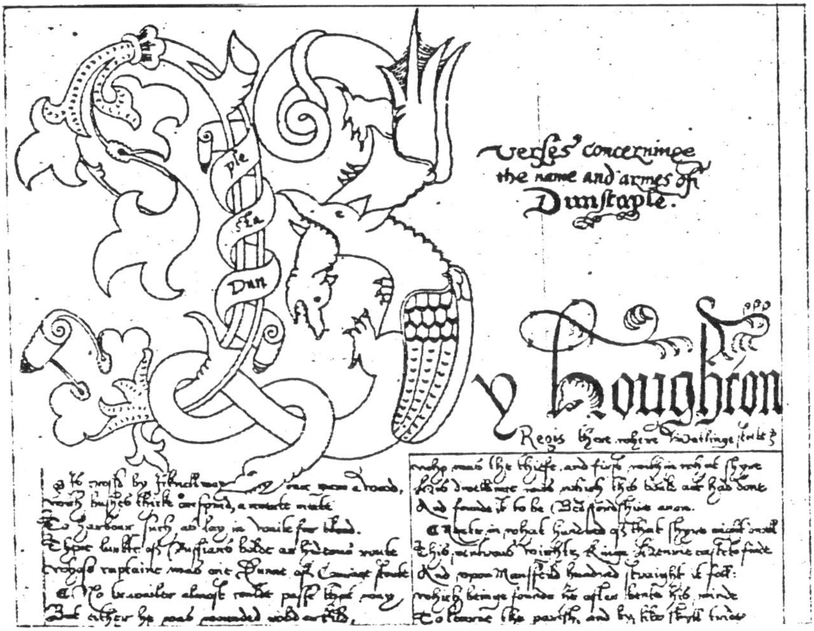

A curate, called John Willis, illustrated the story of Dun The Rober which had been recorded at the Priory around 1280.
(Courtesy; Rector and Church Wardens at the Priory Church of St. Peter)

Most of the original records kept by registrar, Thomas Perkins, appear to have been lost. Either he or one of the incumbents copied a jumble of entries into the book at a later date. The sending of copies to the bishop (Bishop's Transcripts) became illegal; in Dunstable the last list was sent in 1643.

* As registrar, Thomas Perkins signed the register in 1655 and handed over to Bishop Lyster and the church wardens in 1662.

John Willis, who was curate in 1600, drew an elaborate picture on the cover of the register. (Courtesy; the Rector and Church Wardens at the Priory Church of St. Peter)

Burials

No records at all have survived between the end of February 1644 and 1653; then there are four muddled entries. After that (apart from 1663) some, but probably not all, of the burials were entered each year.

Baptisms and Baptists

There are no entries from 24th March 1643* until some unrecorded date when an unknown writer recorded the baptism of three brothers and sisters spread out over seven years. The next entry, dated but still not signed, is – '1656 June 26. At the request of Josias Settle I did writt down the berth of his childerne the same day above writtone'. The list of five children starts with Elkanah, son of Josias – Sar[ha] Settle, born 1st February and baptised 9th February 1648 and ends with Jeremhia born 22nd November 1657 and baptised a week later. This could have been entered by the newly arrived Isaac Bringhurst. Then there is a heading, *'Borne'*, and a family of five births spread between 1646 and 1656.

If a Register did record births between 1653 and 1656, the lists must have been lost because after these three families there are several pages of muddled in-filling. Six more belated births and baptisms are followed by the heading *Baptised* and another twenty-three mixed entries. Then six mixed entries are followed by the heading *Baptised* and another twenty-three very mixed dates – and so it continues.

Some unknown recorder has written a sentence – 'Some Births of children not before Registered borne before the coming of the late Act but Registered, since (by the Parish Register) at the desire and upon the Testimonie of the Parents of the said Children'. This is followed by forty names; twelve were baptised, the rest, presumably, were not.

The earliest, 1626, and the latest, 1672, were possible mistakes. By far the majority are from 1646 to 1654 but the

---

* Until 1752 the church year began on 25 March. This means January, February and most of March appear at the end of the year. With one exception I have used the modern system of dating.

inclusion of one from each year, 1657, 1658 and 1659 rules out the Register being the same person who entered the Settle family baptisms. The next three blocks of names may have been copied from previous records but in 1662 the entries are back to the pre-1642 method, except that the dates are in the wrong order. They include children baptised at four, eight and ten years old. One example of what are, probably, many mistakes, is that of Lydia Groome; she was baptised on 16th September 1662 aged four years but was previously entered as 'born' on 16th March 1657*. From all the above it appears that the ceremony of baptism was available in Dunstable from at least 1647, but that in the 1650s only about twenty percent of the children were baptised. This may mean that less than twenty percent of parents wanted the church ceremony of infant baptism for their children. Had the *Confederates* of 1616 become the core of the new *Baptist movement* of the early 1650s?

Marriages – In the Church and in the Market Place

These continue to be entered in the register until 24th September 1643. Then they come to an abrupt stop and, except for five entries between 1648 and 1653, there are no more traditional entries until 1656. However, in 1654 and 1655 there is a new type of entry; the Register recorded the banns as well as the date of the wedding. The first entry read – 1654 'The intention of Mariage betwixt Thomas Wats and Jane Long (both of Dunstable) was published in the Markett according to ye Act in that behalfe on Sept. 27, Octob. 4, and Octob. 11. They were Maried Novemb. 2, 1654'. But it doesn't say where they were married. Did the magistrate come to the market place every time a couple wanted to get married? On the other hand, these 'Independent Christians of Dunstable' may have been married by one of the lecturers.

According to the register there were six other marriages of this type during 1654 and 1655. In 1656 and 1657 there are a total of seventeen normal entries but only two in 1658; none from 1659 to 1664, two in the early months of 1665 and then no more until September 1671. The same thing happened four more

* This is the one exception made, correcting the dates to the modern practice.

times in the decade. However several of the lists, which were once again being sent to the bishop, have survived – proving that records were being kept somewhere.

After the Restoration

In most parishes the registers were once more kept with reasonable accuracy. One reason for the confusion in Dunstable may have been that the incumbents often lived in Kensworth or that the numerous Baptists in the community preferred to keep their own records.

By law, all marriages now had to be performed in church by an ordained clergyman and couples previously married by a magistrate were supposed to remarry in church. However, some Dunstablians were still arranging for an unofficial civil marriage. Although no marriages were recorded in 1668, when the Archdeacon was at Bedford, on 28th April 1669 he recorded – 'Thomas Hawkins of Dunstable and Mary Harbert Spinster who under pretence of marriage after ye phanatique manner live together in fornication'. Also '. . . they have wholly absented themself from divine servis for 6 months last past'[53].

The Growing Baptist Movement

When, in 1670, the Independents were allowed to license both a meeting house and a leader, there is no mention of Dunstable. But a meeting place, for Baptists, was registered at Kensworth.

Those clergy in the Established Church who had welcomed the Bible, not prayer book, based form of worship, had a difficult time in the early 1660s. They had no choice but to conform or to lose their livings. The leaders and preachers of the Independent movement were in an even worse position. Once again, everybody was obliged by law to attend their own parish church. No man who had not been ordained by a bishop could hold a living or preach in the parish church and no meetings could be held other than in the parish church.

53 Wigfield, W.M. BHRS. Vol. 20.

By the end of the war the Rev. Edward Harrison had become an army chaplain. He returned to Kensworth; although ordained in 1640 as a clergyman in the Church of England, he had become convinced that the baptism of children was wrong. He and his followers believed that members of Christ's church should be men and women who had reached a commitment and who had asked for and received baptism as 'believers'.

Harrison must have been a much respected man and a powerful preacher. By the time that he moved to organise a chain of Baptist meetings in London, his followers came from up to thirty surrounding towns and villages. Miss Bell points out that from these early followers of Edward Harrison came the beginnings of several Baptist congregations in Bedfordshire and Hertfordshire[54]. This was certainly the case with Dunstable.

During the war the group had been kept together by a Kensworth man, Thomas Hayward, and he took over again after 1656. Like John Bunyan, of Bedford, he found himself, even before the coronation of Charles II, in a dangerous and difficult situation. Apart from the problem of trying to keep their groups together when meetings were illegal and attendance could end in prison, they had to make a personal decision. This was whether they should demonstrate the strength of their belief by going to prison or whether to dodge the constables and remain with their persecuted followers.

The Abingdon Association

Sometime around 1650 the leaders of the scattered groups of Baptists took advice from ex-army chaplains such as Edward Harrison and linked themselves into associations. Kensworth joined a very large group based in Oxfordshire. Their messengers (representatives) visited Wormsley, near Watlington, on the 3rd September 1652 and Tetsworth, near Thame, on 17th January 1653[55]. At these meetings they agonized over the lawfulness of marriages between believers and non-believers and whether to

54 Bell, P. Belief in Bedfordshire.
55 Tibbutt, H.G. BHRS. Vol. 51.

refuse membership to those who, once they had become genuine believers, refused to accept a second baptism*. The leaders at these scattered groups often had to make difficult decisions and on the 30th October 1656 a letter was sent to Kensworth asking them to advise and encourage others in their area – 'using the scripture directions and grounds, which the Lord has given you'[56].

A Meeting is Held in Dunstable

On the 16th August 1657 the messengers from Kensworth and Eversholt suggested that, although they would continue to visit Oxfordshire, meetings should also be held in their own area. In January 1658 the Association of Churches of Hertfordshire, Bedfordshire and Buckinghamshire was formed. A meeting was held in Dunstable 'on the 3rd and 4th days of the first month 1659'.

Representatives came from Kensworth, Eversholt, Pirton, [Hemel] Hemsptead, Luton, Stukely [Stewkley], Watford, Newport Pagnell and Bedford. The proceedings started with the recording of recent deaths and the distressing news that from around the area there were members who, despite warnings, refused to attend worship or communion. In some of the churches, including Kensworth, there was a 'sad complaining of much deadness and flatness'. Nevertheless, they thanked God that there was peace amongst them and that despite the deadness and coldness there remained a spirit of integrity and truth towards God. The reasons given by the representatives from Kensworth was that 'the people called Quakers have by craftie instruments much divulged their tenets among them . . .'. They also reported that some of the members at Kensworth were 'sore buffeted with temptations'. However, it was not all bad news. Kensworth was one of the churches which reported that 'some hopeful branches doe appeare among them very comfortably

---

* At Kensworth they felt strongly that this was the correct thing to do, but John Bunyan in the Bedford area and Zachary Symmes in America felt that a strict rule in this matter would damage unity within their groups.

56 White, B.R.(ed) Association Records of the Particular Baptists of England, Wales and Ireland.

growing up as to the worthe of the Lord for whom they desire the prayers of the saints'.

The rest of the business which was discussed concerned problems in other churches where there was a risk of complete breakdown. In most cases it was decided to send a team of messengers to offer help, advice and support on grounds which could be found in scripture and which 'through the blessing of God might be profitable'[57].

This meeting was definitely held in Dunstable rather than in Kensworth, though exactly where is not known. The first surviving register does not start until 1675 and even then titles 'Brother' and 'Sister' replace christian names. It includes members of the Fosse family, who may have been innkeepers, but the visitors probably lodged in the houses of local members. A member of the Finch family played a major role in the scandal of 1616 and there were at least two members at Kensworth. They owned a large barn in West Street which might *possibly* have been used for the meetings.

Several different members represented Kensworth at these early Oxfordshire meetings; Hayward himself went at least twice, while at one of the later meetings Kensworth was represented by the well-known Baptist preacher Benjamin Coxe. He was also present at the meeting in Dunstable[58].

This was not the first meeting to be held in Dunstable, as there are references to an earlier one, but it was probably the last for many years. Charles II returned to London on 29th May 1660 and clergymen who had lost their livings in the early 1640s were ready and waiting to return. The Bishop of Lincoln, whose position had been dissolved in 1642, died in 1658, but on 17th October 1660, a new bishop was installed and during the same month the county magistrates, in Quarter Sessions at Bedford, issued an order 'for the public reading of the liturgy of the Church of England'. In Leighton Buzzard the minister, William Annand, preached in favour of the Book of Common Prayer[59].

---

57 & 58 White, B.R.(ed) Association Records of the Particular Baptists of England, Wales and Ireland.

59 Brown, J. John Bunyan.

A Period of Persecution

It was on the 12th November 1660 that John Bunyan was arrested and from then on the meetings had to be held in secret. During the 1660s an increasing number of 'Dissenters' were arrested for attending what were described as 'unlawful assemblies' or 'conventicles'. Their crime was 'taking part in . . . an excercise of religion not in accordance with the Liturgy or practice of the Church of England'. Fines, periods of imprisonment and even transportation were a real risk for persistent offenders. For the next eight years there are no records and very little information. Hayward decided to avoid the constables and remained with his flock. He was still active when, in 1669, a survey was made of conventicles and their leaders[60].

William III is Crowned and Brings Toleration

In 1689 Mary (daughter of James II) and her husband William came to England and insisted on a policy of toleration. Meeting places, usually private houses or barns, leaders and teachers were all licensed.

Hayward had died in the same year as John Bunyan (1688), which may be why the first surviving record for Kensworth is a licence for the Quakers. 'The House of Thomas Hayward' was registered on the 14th July 1690. There were two families of Haywards in Kensworth; this may have been the house of his widow or son. On his death, Hayward was referred to as 'that laborious servant of Christ'[61]. This inspiring man had gathered together the 'free thinkers' of Kensworth, Dunstable and from many other villages and towns for many miles around. He had encouraged and protected them during the frightening years following the Restoration and had kept his very mixed group of members united. Following his death, Brother Finch and other

60 Wigfield, W.M. BHRS Vol. 20.
61 Baker, R. For the Generation Following.

senior members left Kensworth to attend meetings arranged by Brother Marsom of Luton*.

Gravestones standing in a private orchard at Thorn. These were once adjacent to a Baptist Chapel. (LPE)

A Baptist Church in Dunstable

Some of the Dunstable Baptists left with Marsom but others remained loyal to Kensworth. It is not recorded when they first decided to meet in Dunstable. The present church uses 1675 as the date of their foundation, which is the date of the first surviving register. It includes the names of their Kensworth and Dunstable members and affiliated groups from as far away as Welwyn, St. Albans and Berkhamsted. By 1694 about forty Dunstable names had been entered.

---

* The graveyard at Thorn is all that remains of a small meeting house which Samuel Marsom and others provided in 1749.

It may have been the departure of Brother Marsom and the founding of the new group in Luton which decided the Dunstable Baptists to hold some of their meetings nearer home. An entry in the church register for 1696 records 'Sister Riggs received into full communion at a Church Meeting at Dunstable'[62].

The 'Old Baptist Chapel' which in 1849 replaced an earlier building damaged in a storm. (LPE)

It was in 1707 that their leader, William Brittin (yeoman) of Houghton Regis, John Cooke (joyner) of Dunstable and three others negotiated the purchase of a piece of land at the upper end of Tile Kiln Close (near Butts Lane); the new church was opened in 1775.

62 Baker, R. For the Generation Following.

The People Called Quakers

The soldiers based at Newport Pagnell had the opportunity to listen to some of the finest lecturers of the day. One of these was George Fox. By 1648 he and some friends were holding meetings in north Lancashire and the Lake District. Sometimes they referred to themselves as 'Truth's Friends' or 'The Friends of Truth'. Today they are known as the 'Society of Friends'. They believed that God's truth comes more clearly when a group of friends wait on Him in silence and that individuals 'answer that of God in every one'. In the 17th century some of them felt so strongly that there was no need for intermediaries, such as priests, sacraments and sermons that they were prepared to go into the parish church and attempt to break up the service. The home of Margaret Fell in Ulverston (Lancs) became their base and from there the message was carried all over England.

The Quakers Come to Dunstable

George Fox was constantly travelling and visited Bedfordshire on more than one occasion. However, it was a Lancashire farmer called Richard Hubberthorne who brought the message to Dunstable. He was returning from London and paused to form a small group in the house of John Goodman at Markyate before riding into Dunstable. It was at the end of 1654 or early in 1655 that he preached in the market place near the crossroads. Whatever he said seriously influenced a widow named Elizabeth Chester, whose bakery overlooked that area. Together with her son Edward, she had a prosperous business north of the Nag's Head and their home became the local headquarters for the Quakers. Henry Newman, his son Henry and members of the How and King families from Sewell were all influenced by either Hubberthorne or Chester. Hubberthorne was not the only Quaker preaching in Bedfordshire. John Crook JP, a retired Parliamentary army captain and owner of Beckerings Park (near Ridgemont) was influenced by William Dewsbury, a Yorkshire shepherd. Crook quickly became the teacher and leader of several groups. The survey of 1669 records that he was a visiting teacher at Houghton Regis and six other villages across mid-Bedfordshire[63]. Just as the Baptists travelled out to Kensworth, so the Quakers travelled to Sewell. This was particularly important after the death of Cromwell in September 1657. No reference has been found of Quakers disrupting services in and around Dunstable. However, they were very unpopular: not only with the Baptists who were frightened that they would confuse their members and cause them to drift away, but also with members of the parish church who resented that they refused to pay their church rates and tithes, the clergy because they would not treat the church with respect and lastly the magistrates who were infuriated because Quakers would not take their hats off in court or swear on the Bible. Oliver Cromwell was aware of these complaints but he could see through to the deep beliefs which drove some of the Quakers to extremes. While he was in power they were partly protected. Nevertheless, as early as 1654 the accounts of the headquarters in Kendal include an entry of £1.10s which had been sent to support 'James Lancaster and the rest in Bedford Gaol'. The following year George Fox himself noted that 'the judges were in a great rage in Bedfordshire and many of the magistrates . . .'. He thought that this was because so many of the Quakers refused to attend their parish churches[64].

Edward Chester Tries to Help

It was bad enough for the Baptists, but the fact that the Quakers failed to treat the magistrates with respect meant that they were treated far more severely, at times quite brutally. To try to relieve the men and women left for months, even years in prison for non-payment of heavy fines, local representatives sent the details to a committee in London. In this way money and legal advice could be sent out from the 'Meeting for Sufferings'. Edward Chester became Bedfordshire's first representative. Some of his reports are available for study as they were published in two large volumes, early in the 18th century, entitled *The Sufferings of the People Called Quakers, 1652–1689.*

---

63 Wigfield, W.M. BHRS Vol. 20.
64 Wagon, J.C. Bedfordshire Magazine Vol. 4.

The Quakers Meet at Sewell

Sometime after 1660 the group left Dunstable and held their meetings at hidden sites on Dunstable Downs or on Caddington Common. The only records of the early 1660s to survive are Chester's reports of those in prison.

On one occasion the Earl of Bridgewater (Ashridge House) signed a warrant for the arrest of eighteen men, including Chester, How and Newman senior, who had been rounded up at a meeting just over the Buckinghamshire border. Their case was never heard in court as they refused to swear on oath and were sent to prison. It is possible that their swift release was due to the fact that they were such a large group. Some years later, a group arrested on Caddington Common (near the present A5 road) were sent to the Hertford Assizes and severely punished. When the Archdeacon came to Dunstable in June 1668, he excommunicated Edward Chester (baker), William and Daniel Fossey (grocers), Thomas Halsey (maltster) and Thomas Colard. When he returned in November he excommunicated Henry Newman (husbandman), Robert Kemp (hemp dresser) and four others from the Houghton Regis group. Both groups consistently refused to attend their parish churches.

Despite these attacks and possibly encouraged by George Fox during a visit he made to Luton in 1677, the two groups joined together and on 26th April 1678 they leased a plot of land at Sewell which would be big enough to accommodate a burial ground and a small meeting house. This was first registered in 1689 following the Toleration Act of William and Mary. Edward Chester's house remained their headquarters, but it is not known exactly when the Sewell building was erected. It is doubtful if it was as early as 1678, because in that year Henry Newman (junior) was in gaol for refusing to pay one shilling (5p) towards the repair of All Saints Church, remaining there for two-and-a-half years. John Barton of Studham received a sentence of three-and-a-half years for a similar offence. In 1683 Daniel King of Sewell was imprisoned for his refusal to take the oath of allegiance and remained there for many years. They were amongst friends; between 1664 and 1668 an average of over a hundred men and women from 67 parishes were presented each year at the Assizes[65]. There were far fewer arrests after 1689, but if a Quaker did have to attend court, there was still the possibility of detention for refusal to swear on the Bible. As late as 1696, Daniel King, having stubbornly refused to pay tithes for eight years, had a cow taken in lieu of payment[66].

The Burial Ground at Sewell

It was not only local people who were buried at Sewell. the parish register for Houghton Regis records several members of the Chester family as 'buried at Sewell', as were residents of many surrounding towns and villages. John Crook (who spent time in a

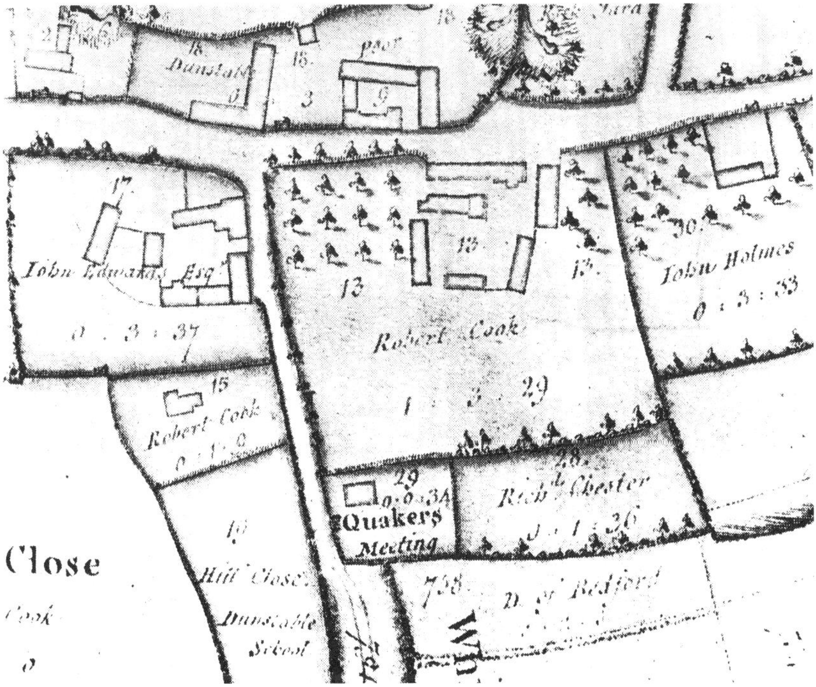

A small section of the map produced for the Duke of Bedford in 1762, showing the position of the Quaker Meeting House at Sewell.

65 Godber, J. History of Bedfordshire.
66 Wagon, J.C. Bedfordshire Magazine Vol. 13, No. 97.

London prison) was eventually driven out of Beckerings Park to live in Hertfordshire, from where he wrote to his 'Friends of Sewell Meeting' just before his death in 1699, when he was brought to Sewell for burial.

A Quaker Meeting House in Dunstable

Once it was possible to register a building as a place of worship, the Dunstable Quakers began once more to meet at Edward Chester's house. In 1712 a meeting house was built in West Street with a small burial ground at the rear[67]. It was closed in 1797, the site being cleared and re-used by 1850. Although nothing remains of the meeting house at Sewell, details of its later history are recorded by John Wagon in *Bedfordshire Magazine Volume 13*.

Edward Chester, who welcomed the Quakers, lived in the bakery north of the Nag's Head. (LPE)

67 Godber, J. Friends in Bedfordshire and West Hertfordshire, quoted by Benson, N. Dunstable in Detail.

Chapter 6

An Important New Industry Comes to Dunstable

Day to Day Life

The income which was brought to Dunstable, and to other towns and villages which lay alongside main roads, had to be balanced by the problems; at a time of civil war these outweighed the profits. Unwanted visitors brought infection, robbed the market and bought supplies in the king's name, paid for with official chits – almost too much trouble to redeem. As late as October 1647 Joseph Smythe was trying to get the committee for sequestrations to let him draw the money he was owed direct from the tenants of Royalist Spencer Potts of Chalgrave, who in turn owed their rents to the committee[68]. Smythe may have been an innkeeper, as at different times in the mid 17th century members of the family owned both The Bull and The Saracen's Head.

The War Brought Changes in Political Education

One of the few good things to come about as a result of the bitterly contested civil war was a general improvement in literacy. No doubt many of the soldiers who returned home from the war enjoyed reading stories, from the Bible, to their children and grandchildren. Also those soldiers who had taken part in the fighting would have been able to recount stories of the great battles they had experienced and to argue, in a more informed way, about religion and politics.

---

68 The Calendar of the County Committee for Compounding, No. 1592.

Apart from the fact that the war of the 17th century was fought because of men's beliefs, not their desire for property and territory, it had more in common with the 15th century Wars of the Roses than with the 20th century fighting in France. Detachments from both armies moved around the country attacking castles known to be disloyal to their cause. From time to time armies met and then there was a major battle, as at Edgehill in 1642. On occasions, one army would actually stalk the other from village to village as at Naseby[69]. For the majority of soldiers the horror of face-to-face fighting was not continuous, there were long periods of inactivity. For weeks, sometimes for months, soldiers lived out, billeted in those counties which supported their cause, or else living in garrisons, such as at Newport Pagnell. To help them with their reading, their understanding of biblical stories, their appreciation and understanding of Parliamentary and military policies, regular lectures and periods of discussions were arranged at the garrison.

Both sides were deeply religious; regular services were held and many of the extremely Puritan free-thinking clergymen who had lost their livings at the time of Archbishop Laud became army chaplains. Some of these went even further than the reforming Puritans and wanted to get rid of the Church of England altogether. From this position some of them moved on to embrace what we would think of as socialist, even extreme socialist, policies. These Parliamentary chaplains prided themselves that, when they had the opportunity, they would preach to civilians as well as to soldiers. Their political ideas, of working towards a more level and fair society, where education and training for work would be available to all men and women, were carried all over the country.

Another political theme which spread rapidly (and developed into a movement where followers were known as *the Diggers*) was that unused, and apparently unwanted, common land should be made available for low paid workers to grow their own food. 'Commons' were pieces of open land which were part of the

---

69 Evans, V. Folk.

landowners' estates and the efforts of the Diggers were bitterly resented and resisted*. As many of the political leaders visited the garrison of Newport Pagnell, it can be assumed that some of them came through Dunstable and may have 'lectured' in the Priory Church.

The Diggers

On Sunday 1st April 1649, a group of labourers gathered on St. George's Hill, at Walton-on-Thames, and began to dig up the waste land to make allotments. There were about twenty or thirty of these *Diggers* but they boasted that there would soon be four or five thousand. The authorities interpreted their actions not as a genuine attempt to get land but as a political demonstration. The Justices were egged on by the frightened landowners; law cases and attacks by vandals caused the Diggers to move to nearby Cobham Heath. Attacks by organised vandals continued and the colony was disbanded by April 1650, although they did try to hang on as a centre for the other groups which had spontaneously sprung up in the counties around London and in the Midlands.

Intriguing Comments by Walter Blythe

In 1649, Walter Blythe, 'a lover of Ingenuity', published a book concerning the improvement of arable farming in England. He included an account of his travels to try and persuade English landowners to try out his ideas. He wrote about the need to improve the yield of cereals, the need to increase the amount of land capable of growing cereals and the advantages and disadvantages of enclosing common land. He then went on to give as an example:

> 'there are many hundreds if not thousands of Acres of Lands near *Dunstable*, in a Valley under *Puddle, or Chalke-Hills*, just under the bottome of the Hills (an eminent place knowne well to most)

---

* The history of the Levellers and the Diggers can be found in many specialist books especially Hill, C. The World Turned Upside Down.

> [travellers] which I believe runs both wayes farre, but on both sides the Rode-way to Coventry and West Chester the Land lyeth, with a little Brooke, or streame running through it; All which Lands if you observe them above halfe the yeare lye full of water, if not under water, and I believe is worth about five shillings an Acre, I am sure abundance of it is not worth three shillings, and some not worth two shillings an Acre, which if my Judgement faile not, may easily be drayned, and laid to sound and wholsome [i.e. useful land]'*.

He then went on to discuss different methods of drainage, in particular using the stream to take away the storm water which used to pour off Puddle Hill. He predicted that if his methods were carried out the improvement would be so great that the land would be dry enough to produce a crop of hay.

Blythe then made some remarks, the meaning of which we can only guess. The possibility of draining this piece of waste land

Aerial view looking down on the modern communities at Chalk Hill and Sewell, illustrating the low lying ground on either side of the road. (OR)

---

* I have modernised the letter 'S'.

The cover of Walter Blythe's book, printed at the Kings Head, in the 'Old Bayley', in 1652.

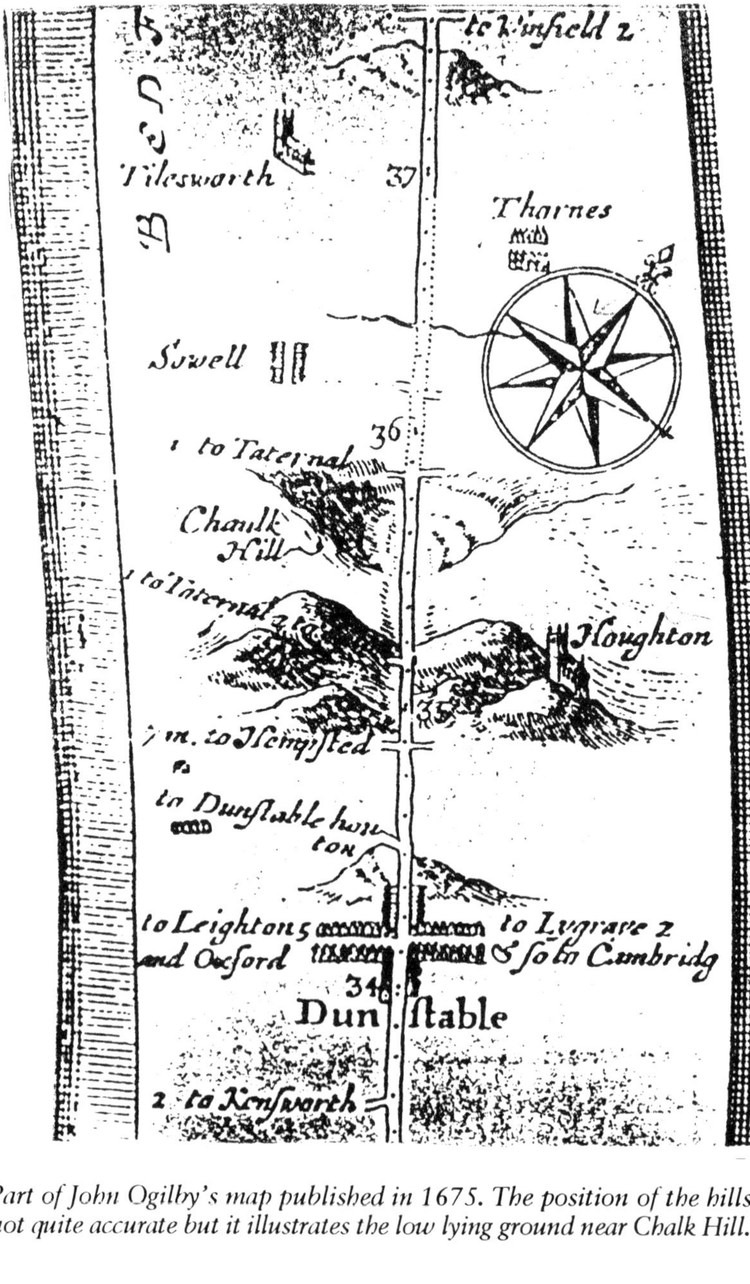

Part of John Ogilby's map published in 1675. The position of the hills is not quite accurate but it illustrates the low lying ground near Chalk Hill.

and bringing it into cultivation was quite obvious – 'and this offer of Improvement was once tendred [tendered] to them, [the landowners] who could not agree there in, but made many . . . objections . . . although it was offered them to be done at another's cost and charge . . .'70 [i.e. this would have been done at no cost to the owners]. John Ogilby's road map of 1675 and several 18th century county maps clearly mark the Holyhead road (Watling Street) passing over the Chalk Hill and also the quite big stream which crosses the road just north of the hill. The aerial view of the area, taken by Omer Roucoux, shows how flat the fields are; in the foreground, the land on one side is used for sewage treatment. On the other side of the road it is now cultivated.

Ownership of the land is less clear. One side of the road, the part of Houghton Regis known as Thorn, was owned by the Ashridge Estate and wasn't sold to Henry Brandreth until c1654. On the other side Sewell had been sequestered from Royalist leader, Sir Lewis Dyve; Henry Brandreth bought that side of Houghton Regis c1652. Who were the people who had previously offered to drain the land? Could they have been a group of Diggers?

The Diggers Come to Dunstable

Even before the Diggers made their attempt to cultivate the waste land at Walton, there were other scattered attempts to make more land available to the very poor and to the unemployed. In Buckinghamshire attempts had been made to break open private enclosures so that the land could once again be used by a larger number of people. Enthusiasts travelled from group to group, pamphlets were printed and distributed; messengers carried them to places like Dunstable where the people were known to be sympathetic. The Diggers were one group within a much larger party known as *Levellers* who had had a big meeting at Aylesbury, in the first week of May 1649. In Dunstable there must have been sufficient support for these different ideas for them to be discussed openly in the inns. One Leveller idea, civil marriage, was happily accepted in Dunstable; the placing of higher

---

70 Blythe, W. The English Improver.

courts under the control of Parliament rather than the church would also have been popular. Removal of the market tolls, which at the time favoured towns like Dunstable but damaged country people, wouldn't have been so popular; nor in a town so desperately short of land for growing food would the idea of sharing what little they did have appeal to the richer members of the community. However the great majority were not rich and many of them would have been desperately keen to get a small allotment. The idea of allowing them to cultivate unused land outside the parish boundary probably appealed to rich and poor alike.

In the spring of 1650, when the settlement at Cobham Heath was really under pressure and was desperately short of both food and money, the leader and twenty-one of the members sent out an appeal for help. Two messengers carried this letter to settlements in many counties north of London *and one of the places that they visited was Dunstable*[71].

The Struggle for Economic Recovery

The dangerous roads, the shortage of food and almost absence of horses for hire made it a particularly difficult time for innkeepers. Even after the Battle of Naseby there were sporadic outbreaks of fighting and it was probably the mid 1650s before trade really began to improve. However, once the roads were really safe, people began to travel again both for business reasons and for pleasure. In 1657 one of the first stage coach services in England began to run through Dunstable and prosperity was once more a possibility. A new form of tax, based on the number of hearths in each house, (see below) reinforces our picture of this prosperity.

At the end of the Civil War England was very short of small coinage and until copper coins were introduced nationally in 1672 many traders produced their own tokens. It is thought that they were struck locally using a simple mill and screw process, the dies for the presses being manufactured in London[72]. A large

71 Hill, C. The World Turned Upside Down.
72 Hogg, R. and G. Markyate's Past. No. 3.

number of these Dunstable tokens have survived and they are of great interest because they often carry information greater than just the name of the man for whom they were made.

Trade Tokens Were Issued

Not only is it possible, by combining the hearth tax figures with other types of records, to identify around twenty of the even greater number of inns and beerhouses but we can also recognise a carrier and five forges. From other sources we know that there was at least one brasier, leather worker, saddler and collarmaker. Several innkeepers were once again specialising in keeping horses for hire; there were facilities for stage coaches, private coaches and for more humble travellers. By 1680 Henry Sam had registered the White Horse as one of Bedfordshire's first post offices.

Nathaniel Wimpew had his sign of the White Hart on one side of his token and a mitre on the other. It is thought that he may have been the son of William Wimpew, a prebendary of Lincoln Cathedral who was at the Priory in 1671*. It is not surprising that William Fossey, landlord of the Red Lion, should have a White Swan on his token as that was the previous name of the inn[73]. What is surprising is the similarity to the Gold Swan brooch found in the Friary Field in 1965[74].

The trade token of William Wimpew of the White Hart showing the mitre.

* I am grateful to Miss Sheila Furnell for pointing out this information.
73 Benson, N. Dunstable in Detail.
74 Evans, V. Dunstable with the Priory, 1100–1550.

A trade token of William Fossey – a white swan with a chain.

Several other tokens have been found which, combined with the Hearth Tax records, help us to identify some of Dunstable's leading businesses, e.g. Edward Chester, baker (4 hearths), Daniel Finch, merchant (2 hearths), John Whitely, draper (2 hearths)[75]. Other sources of this period introduce us to Thomas Foxton, butcher (Robert and Thomas both had 3 hearths), John Eames (7 hearths) who had hats stolen from his wagon and Thomas Chapman, barber-surgeon (2 hearths) who had recently bought The Bell which is now part of The Saracen's Head.

The Dunstable Swan Jewel, showing chain. (OR)

75 Marshall, L. BHRS, Vol. 16.

We will find later on in this book that many new businesses opened as a response to the expanding travel industry. No doubt morale also improved and by the time that Charles II died in 1685, Dunstable was once more a vibrant and successful business centre.

Wider Horizons

During the Civil War officers, recruits and pressed men continually rode or marched across England. Quite apart from the horrors of war, many of them experienced situations which were entirely new to them. To many of the pressed men from rural Bedfordshire, who were not even familiar with Bedford or St. Albans, London must have seemed like a foreign country. The businessmen of Dunstable were used to travelling and sometimes married the daughters of business contacts in other parts of England. The landed gentry often of course arranged marriages amongst their own kind in other parts of England but on the whole even those who regularly travelled to the Inns of Court or Westminster were unaware of the wild and beautiful scenery in other parts of England. The travel industry, which had begun to build up in the late 16th century but had been brought to an abrupt halt with the outbreak of war, now began to grow extremely rapidly.

Private Coaches Were Regularly Seen in Dunstable

Most people still preferred to travel on horseback but increasingly the richer families began to buy or hire coaches. When the senior civil servant, Samuel Pepys, began his diary in the mid 1660s, he was in the habit of hiring a coach to take his wife on a country outing. In 1668 he fulfilled a long-held ambition and commissioned one for himself. The novelty of this impressive purchase excited him so much that he would drop into the coachmaker's yard, on his way home from the office, to watch the progress of the work. He resolved to have the standards of his coach 'gilt with this new sort of varnish, which will come but to 40 shillings'. He was not the only one to call in and watch the coachmakers at work; he met there people of his acquaintance.

Pepys does not mention Dunstable, but from his description of visits elsewhere we can tell that during the second half of the 17th century it was the done thing for upper civil servants and officials connected with the court to spend their Sundays sightseeing and relaxing at interesting scenic places thirty to forty miles out of London. It was usually necessary to have a very early start, a breakfast stop and a comfortable inn at their destination. They could be away from home for eighteen hours or more, so would hire a private room at the inn and settle down for an afternoon sleep. On arrival Pepys would attend the morning service; later he would talk with friends and acquaintances, do some sightseeing and go for quite a long walk.

When he took his wife and some friends to Epsom in July, 1667, they left home at 5.00am. They were travelling in a coach drawn by four horses and, having packed some wine, beer and a cold fowl, no breakfast stop was necessary. They arrived at 8.00am, booked a room at the inn, settled themselves in and Pepys went on his own to church. There he saw, and noted in his diary, so many courtiers and officials like himself that there may have been an element of 'seeing and being seen' in these Sunday outings. After church he returned to his party and found that they were dissatisfied with their room. The landlord kindly 'borrowed' a room for them which suggests that some private families might have been prepared to supplement their income by letting out a private parlour to a respectable visiting family. After dinner the whole party had a nap before going out to explore.

As far as Dunstable is concerned, the interesting part of their sightseeing was the walk which the whole party took over Epsom Downs. There they met a shepherd watching his sheep while listening to stories from the Bible, read to him by his young son. While the ladies picked one of the prettiest nosegays that Pepys had ever seen, he talked to the shepherd. In particular, he commented on the man's 'woolen knit stockings of two colours mixed and his shoes shod with iron both at the toe and heels, and with great nails in the soles of his feet . . .'[76].

The shepherd described the Downs as being full of stones (flints) explaining why the metal protection was necessary. He must have illustrated this by hitting a few flints with his crook because Pepys did then 'try to cast stone with his [the shepherd's] horne crooke'. This outing could so easily have been based in Dunstable that, even if Pepys did not come himself, Dunstable must have hosted similar Sunday outings. Lambourne describes the Dunstable shepherds, cutting and carving walking sticks for the entertainment of the people who climbed up over Dunstable Downs to visit them[77].

The Earl of Bedford Visits Dunstable

The great country landowners who could afford a house in London as well as an estate in Bedfordshire already had one or more coaches. If the roads were bad when they set out for the London season, the party from Woburn would spend their first night in Dunstable or St. Albans. It was impossible for four horses to pull the loaded coaches over Puddlehill, so they regularly hired a 'cock-horse' from the man at the bottom of the hill for 6 pence (2 1/2p), to supply the extra pulling power.

The male members of the household, male servants and even some of the maids rode horseback. The smaller trunks, two of which cost 15 shillings (75p) in 1681, travelled, under the seats, inside the coach with the ladies and their maids. The 'portmantle' trunks (18 shillings each in 1694) were tied outside or travelled separately on a wagon or on the carrier's cart. The female servants who were not able to ride sometimes travelled with the trunks. Coach hire for two house maids, plus their expenses on the road, cost 14s.6d in 1685. At this date The Sugar Loaf had not risen to become sufficiently high class to be patronised by the household; they normally stayed at The Crown[78].

Heavy four-wheeled coaches were kept for these family

76 The Diary of Samuel Pepys
77 Lamborn, C. Dunstaplelogia.
78 Scott Thompson, G. Life in a Noble Household.

journeys. When the first outriders riding into the town were recognised, the word quickly went round from courtyard to courtyard. By the time that the Earl himself appeared with the coach carrying his family, the streets were lined with hopeful residents. These were not professional beggars, they were Dunstablians who lined up with their children and babies as a show of respect for their local earl. Even before he became Lord of the Manor, representing the king's interest in the town, he was known to be generous with his tips. If they knew in time, the bell ringers would run to the church and welcome him with a peal of bells.

Hawking on the Downs

The Earl was very fond of hawking and one of his highest paid outdoor servants was the head falconer. This privileged servant had a small permanent staff and, when needed, two or three footmen were recruited to help him. One of his favourite places for hawking was Dunstable Downs. It was probably the lighter coaches which were used on these occasions, plus game carts and wagons. On the outward journey the procession may have turned off the Holyhead Road and followed a green lane across to West Street but at the end of the day they rode into the centre of the town. The expeditions were planned well in advance because in the evenings the Earl would entertain his guests to a great dinner at The Crown or The White Hart.

When the party rode back into the town after the day's sport on the Downs, they were welcomed with pealing bells and with crowds of cheering people. Women with their own and borrowed children took up their positions around the door of the inn, men and boys jostled each other in the courtyard for the chance to hold a horse or help a tired rider to dismount. Local musicians gathered in the kitchen and tried to persuade the landlord to let them into the dining room – or if not the dining room, the outbuilding where the Earl's servants were entertained.

These servants all wore a distinctive brown and orange livery; when the falconers were working they wore a special uniform, hat and a safety glove which cost 1 shilling. The hawks wore bells and coloured hoods and the whole procession must have been very colourful. In 1689, they were either led to, or met at, the inn by trumpeters. The entry in the account book for that particular visit reads: 'The expenses of his lordship, with his retinue, in August 1689, at Dunstable, with 19s.0d given to servants, ringers and several poor there, and with £1.10s.0d given to music and trumpeters, etc., [paid] at the abbey. £8.8s.0d.' This 19 shillings was reckoned in the day's expenses and possibly paid to the landlord for distribution at his door[79].

Although on Wednesday 9th April 1684 at the General Quarter Sessions of the Peace held at Bedford, the *maximum* yearly wage for a bailiff in charge of a unit was only £5.10 shillings and for a coachman £3.10 shillings these figures were ignored by the great landowners[80]. In 1678, the Earl of Ailesbury, at nearby Houghton House, paid his coachman £6.13s.4d a year plus a winter cloak and a pair of shoes costing 14s.6d. The grooms were paid £5 per year and the postillions £4[81].

Other Important People Visit Dunstable

Several important meetings and visits have already been mentioned in this book. The suitability of Dunstable's good inns and stables, together with its central position, probably means that the recorded visits are only a tiny proportion of the whole. It is recorded, amongst the State Papers, that on 4th May Duke Ormond and his party, who were travelling south to London, broke their journey in Dunstable. He was to wait there and meet Sir George Lane. Semi secret meetings concerning political and religious problems in Ireland have already been mentioned in Chapter 2 of this book. Both these gentlemen were deeply involved in Irish affairs and this may have been the reason for their meeting.

Again, from the State Papers – on 5th August 1673, a Mr Ferguson wrote from Dunstable to his wife at Clerkenwell

79 Scott Thompson, G. Life in a Noble Household.
80 BHRS, Vol. 25, T.S.Willan. A Bedfordshire Wage Assessment of 1684.
81 BHRS, Vol. 32, The Earl of Cardigan, Domestic Expenses of a Nobleman's Household, 1678.

Close. He thanked her for her kindness in seeing him off by the coach. August should have been a good time to travel but he recounted that because the roads were 'so watery and deep' they had had to drive hard to arrive by 8pm.

The Royal Mail

Throughout the centuries, messengers were one of the commonest groups of travellers to be seen passing through Dunstable. Whether they were from an earl's house in London, carrying messages to his steward in the country, or from an abbot or sheriff carrying messages to the king; whether they carried messages concerning trade, government of family affairs, they were a recognised service industry and carried out essential business on behalf of their employers. Their speed depended on the quality of their horses, the natural hazards of the road and also the respect or fear in which they held their employer. Working unsupervised and often very far from home, there were many opportunities for idleness or for taking on a second paid 'message'.

During the reign of Henry VIII, a team of official 'post-boys' was appointed to carry messages up and down the Holyhead Road, heading for London or the Northwest, Wales, Scotland and Ireland. They wore uniform, carried a royal pass and had the legal right to demand private horses, ride then at a careless and often dangerous speed and then leave them at the next stage, twelve or fifteen miles up the road, for the owner to recover. The owners were supposed to claim a fee via the exchequer. Nobody except the Royal Family or those on Parliamentary business, with permission from the monarch or his staff, was supposed to use these messengers.

Private people sent messages by friends, business contacts and professional travellers, e.g. drovers or itinerant salesmen. It was a recognised part of a carrier's job to carry messages and parcels along his route. James I saw the financial possibilities of opening up the Royal Mail so that businesses and private individuals were able to make use of the service. However, the unofficial network of mail carriers continued and stories have been passed down of an unofficial sorting office in a St. Albans inn. Coach drivers, wagoners and carriers got together and swapped the letters which they were carrying, to get them on to the correct route. The fact that people felt that this hit and miss method was preferable to the Royal Mail, shows that it was either considered too expensive, too slow or too unreliable.

If private people were going to use the Royal Mail, post offices were essential. An official broad sheet, published in July 1669, gave [Little] Brickhill as the main post office for Bedfordshire. As late as 1680, the gentry of Bedford were requesting an official postal service between Brickhill and Bedford. In the Post Office archive, the first surviving reference to a Dunstable post office is the collection of bills for 1687 but there must have been one long before that.

It Was Safer to Travel as a Group

The cost of hiring a coach on those few occasions when it was needed was of course cheaper than keeping one throughout the year. However, if travelling very far, it was necessary to take a male relative or servant as an outrider. Travellers who owned their own riding or coach horses could probably afford the time to wait at an inn, such as The Peacock, Islington, on the outskirts of London, and join up with a convoy. The State Papers record that on 21st May 1697 the Justices and the Chancellor of Ireland set out up the Holyhead Road; they were proposing to spend their first night in Dunstable. They were 'accompanied out of town by divers persons of quality'. The inns of Dunstable must have been very full that night!

The Stage Coach Service

A few years before the outbreak of the Civil War, an experiment had been tried of running public coaches, with a set timetable, between London, St. Albans and then on to Cambridge. Had there been no war the idea would no doubt have spread across the country. As it was, a public notice in the newspaper,

Mercurius Politicus, dated 9th April 1657, guaranteed an income for Dunstable that would last for over 175 years.

Presumably representatives of the three entrepreneurs who had inserted the advert, had previously visited Dunstable. If so, the news would have spread all over the town that regular coaches, full of passengers, would soon be stopping there. The notice stated that for the 'convenient accommodation of passengers from and betwixt London and West Chester there is provided several stage coaches, which go from the George Inn without Aldersgate upon every Monday, Wednesday and Friday to Coventry in 2 days for 25 shillings, Stone in 3 days for 30 shillings, Chester in 4 days for 35 shillings. Return on the same day with fresh horses each day'. Timetables were published, cross-routes established and both the standard of inns and the surface of roads were improved, but still the long distance coaches found it very difficult to increase their average speed. As long as they were tied to a system of 'fresh horses every day' there was little chance of improvement. Except in the worst of emergencies, they must struggle on every evening to the appointed town before they could change their exhausted horses. By that time, their dispirited passengers required not only food but a proper night's sleep before they could continue.

However one chose to travel, it was necessary to add overnight accommodation and a series of tips at every stage. No doubt the group of businessmen had hoped that they could stick to their timetable in good weather, even if there were delays during the winter. In practice, travelling at the speed of the slowest horse and, apart from emergencies, only changing horses once in twenty-four hours, there were frequent delays. Weather permitting, they set out two hours before it was properly daylight and stayed on the road another two hours after it began to get dark, but even then, Dunstable, which was normally one night's stop out of London, was quite often the second.

Not for another century, with the mail coach system of changing horses every twelve to fifteen miles, was there really an improvement. Once this happened the speeds were so much increased that overnight stops were unnecessary. Meanwhile the stagecoach system was an excellent idea; there would be a set timetable and each of the stops would be at an inn. Respectable travellers could stable their horse at the inn, settle down by the fire and wait for the coach. A lady could book two seats and travel quite safely across the country with only a maid to help and chaperone her.

Nevertheless, however much the proprietors and regular travellers wanted to improve the roads, there was very little that they could do.

The Roads Cause Problems

People living in 17th century Dunstable probably complained as much about the roads as we do today. There may not have been juggernauts blocking the crossroads, but with two ponds, a blacksmith's forge, two small inns and a large private house all standing in the middle of the road between the Sugar Loaf and the crossroads, they must have been familiar with the problem of congestion. Just as Ashton Square has become a walkway on the west side of Middle Row, leaving High Street South as the main traffic route (A5), so the east side of North Street near the crossroads may have been a narrow slip road, while the wider west side was the main Holyhead Road.*

Delivery vans can today cause hazards by blocking the pedestrian's view, but the worst they leave behind is a patch of oil. A tethered horse could deposit its steaming pile of manure and then move on to the next stop, its driver quite unconcerned about the gentlemen's boots and the ladies' skirts which would come in contact with the mess. Drovers were supposed to bypass the crossroads with their herds of cattle and flocks of sheep, thousands of which came south through Dunstable every year. However, many of these did come straight through the town centre, particularly on market day.

It has been suggested that the iron wheels of farmers' carts and stage coaches, the lumbering timber and stone-carrying carts, the metal shoes worn by horses all striking against the

---

* See frontispiece.

flint-covered roads, mixed with a variety of horns, the noise of frightened animals and the shouting and swearing of drivers and drovers, made a cacophony of sounds almost comparable with those of today.

The First Parish Rate

Within the town, teams of road menders and crossing sweepers could keep the roads in a fit state to allow vehicles and pedestrians to pass in all but the worst of weather. It was the roads on either side of the actual town, which were considered a national scandal and caused so much worry and expense to the townspeople.

Always a difficult geographical area in which to keep good roads, they got much worse during the first half of the 17th century. This was a general deterioration, right across the country, so in 1655, and with revised versions over the next few years, a system of parish rates and 'voluntary' labour was conceived.

As there were no local civil servants, the new scheme was put into the hands of the annual church meeting known as the Easter Vestry. Each year two Surveyors of the Roads (often called Stone Wardens) were 'elected'. They had to see that each household gave up six days a year to mending the roads and that those who owned a horse and cart supplied them. Labour, horses and carts were free but tools had to be bought and there were continual bills from the blacksmiths and wheelwrights. This was because the workmen, who seldom if ever used the roads, did not take their duties very seriously. The money to pay for the road scheme was raised by levying a 'stone rate' from householders, who were assessed on the value of their house. The untrained surveyors had to calculate how much money they would need for the next twelve months and assess the rates.

They then had to get these checked and authorised by the local magistrate, who would support them if householders refused to pay. It was a most unpopular position, especially if the weather made the roads worse than usual; they then might have to claim a second, or even a third, stone rate during the year. The books which they kept are extremely interesting, but unfortunately those for Dunstable are missing.

The Terrible Road North of Dunstable

Although the situation was poor all over the country, locally conditions were particularly bad. In summer, heavy wagons ground the chalk to a fine powder and in winter, rain water drained off the hills on to the clay just north of the town. Once the north-bound traffic left Dunstable, they had to climb over the chalk hill and then drop down and pass through Hockliffe, which received the rain water from the Brickhills.

The very experienced traveller, Celia Fiennes, has given us an excellent description of this piece of road[82]. She was riding south from Warwickshire to London, during the summer of 1697, and approached Dunstable via Woburn and Hockliffe. She travelled along 'a sad road called Hockley in the Hole as full of deep slows [muddy places], in the winter it must be impassable, there is a good pitch'd Causey for foote people and horse that is raised up high from the Road, and a very steepe chaulky hill from whence it has its name the Chalk Hill just as you enter Dunstable'.

The Turnpike Trusts

On 23rd February 1662 'A Bill for Repairing and Maintaining of the Highway called Watling Street in the County of Bedford' had its first reading in Parliament. A committee was set up but Parliament was dissolved before it had time to report. A similar bill was introduced two years later but did not get a second reading. This may be because the previous year an experiment had been allowed at three sites on the Great North Road, including Wadesmill in Hertfordshire. Justices of the Peace were to supervise the collection of tolls for repairing that important piece of road. This experiment uncovered many problems but showed that the method could be successful.

In the next few years, more toll gates were erected and a system developed whereby a group of 'gentlemen' would form a Turnpike Trust, to repair a measured piece of road. They would then get a private Act of Parliament to enable them to collect tolls from travellers, to use on the named piece of road. One of the first, in 1706, was to repair the road, north of Hockliffe, towards

---

82 Hillaby, J. The Journeys of Celia Fiennes.

Stony Stratford. In 1720 The Puddlehill Trust was formed from Hockliffe back to Dunstable. These two trusts were particularly successful and will be discussed in the next book in this series.

From the point of view of the private traveller, one of the great advantages of mail coaches would be that they carried an armed guard! In addition to the delays, the lack of springs under the coaches, the ruts in the roads and the prospect of being enclosed for days at a time with all types of smelly, garrulous, snoring, over-friendly or generally unpleasant travellers, was the fear of armed robbery.

The Highwaymen

The traditional highwayman with a well-cut coat, expensive hat, well-bred horse and valuable case of pistols actually represents the ex-soldiers, usually Royalists, of the Civil War period. By 1646 many young supporters of King Charles I found themselves without home, income or occupation. They made use of what they had – their horse and their pistols.

An Incident at the Five Bells of Stanbridge

One of the best local examples of soldiers turning to highway robbery occurred in 1670. This exciting story is based on fact and took place long before the inn received its present name and status. Like many of our present inns it started as a private house where the owner, in this case Thomas Doggett, had a licence to brew and sell beer.

Local justices Sir St. John Chernock of Hulcote and Thomas Snagg, of Marston Morteyne, met on 6th May 1670. They were told by Daniel Ellingham, yeoman, that on the previous day another yeoman, James Janes of Tilsworth, had reported seeing three men, whom he suspected of a mail coach robbery, crossing Tilsworth fields. They were heading towards Doggett's alehouse, at Stanbridge. Ellingham had at once informed the local constable who appealed to the men of Tilsworth to help him carry out an arrest. So the constable, Ellingham and several local men, carrying staves and weapons, went across the fields to Tilsworth.

Details from an illustrated menu produced in the 1950s for the Five Bells of Stanbridge. (Courtesy of the present owners.)

Very sensibly they went first to the barn at the back of the inn to remove the robber's horses. Instantly the three suspects came out to the barn and demanded to know what was going on. They then drew their pistols and two of them fired at the constable and his assistants, one shot breaking the jaw of a man called Thomas Clarke. Luckily the other pistol did not go off. The third man drew his sword and plunged at a Tilsworth man, called Thomas Beckley, who, as he fell to his knees, said that he was dying. This statement obviously frightened the swordsman, who managed to free one of the horses and escape. This confusion gave the constable the chance to arrest one of the suspects but the third man again used his pistol, presumably firing over the constable's head. This third suspect was eventually arrested but was apparently wounded in the struggle because he died two hours later.

It turned out that their leader was John Fox, a member of the 'Dukes Troope Gard'; he was the man who had shot Clarke so he was taken to Bedford prison. His two friends were a Mr Willobye and Mr Hongerford. The three of them had come north out of London and were suspected of attacking a stage coach near Dunstable. It was later discovered that the three had been hiding at a widow's alehouse in Hockliffe and that the reason for their flight across the fields was because a post boy, who called at the alehouse, had recognised Hongerford's mare. It was one that had been stolen during the raid on the mail coach[83]. Apart from Clarke who, because of his serious injuries, may have been one of the Stanbridge people entered as being on 'constant alms', all the others appear in the Hearth Tax returns of 1671. James Janes was constable in 1671 and this was probably why he made the report. The alehouse in Hockliffe is not known. Several widows are listed in 1671 Hockliffe; the Doggett family owned an inn called the Cock, north of the turn to Woburn. It was used by drovers before they took over, but by 1670 it was rising in status.

This true highwayman story is typical of many which occurred all over England. Later in the 17th century and during the 18th century robbery became an all too common experience.

---

83 BCRO, HSA/1670/W33–4.

Chapter 7

The Century Closes

Towards the end of the 16th century, the people of Dunstable were adapting to life in a town which was no longer dominated by the Augustinian Priory. Trades-people and retailers were making a successful living supplying goods and services not only for wealthy London commuters but also increasingly for travellers.

The decades passed, problems appeared, grew and eventually led to the horrors of civil war. Not only did business suffer badly but the early developing travel industry came to an end. Even when the war was over, the future must have looked very gloomy to the many Dunstablians whose businesses had been damaged by war and who were still overburdoned by taxes. Anyone putting forward ambitious plans and trying to build up capital to invest in a modernised travel industry must have seemed wildly optimistic – but in a surprisingly short time they were proved to be right!

Private travellers on horseback and increasingly in coaches arrived in the town tired, dirty and often far from well as a result of their difficult and dangerous journeys. they were no longer satisfied with poor quality food and communal accommodation; they were looking for somewhere reliably safe, clean and comfortable where they could rest and restore their strength. Dunstable businessmen were ready and able to invest in this exciting, new, high-class industry and their confidence was confirmed when a public notice in the newspaper, Mercurius Politicus, dated 9th April 1657, guaranteed an income for Dunstable that would last for over 175 years.

These early coaches had neither springs nor proper windows but, despite the discomfort, the dangers and the unreliability, stage coaches were soon running all over the country. Innkeepers were only too anxious to sign contracts and become part of this important new industry. Luckily we have direct evidence of Dunstable's recovery, the success of those who responded to the needs of these high-class travellers and the 'spin-off' which spread to blacksmiths, wheelwrights, saddlers, food producers, retailers, and the makers of souvenirs.

When the Priory closed, the innkeepers, backed by money from London businessmen, had been more than ready to take on the commercial side of the travel business, but no plans were made to accommodate the poor, the sick and the numerous vagrants.

The old hospital on the southern boundary remained open for nearly a century. It acted as a district refuge for the care of the sick and was supported by public subscription[84]. A house in West Street was put into the hands of the 'Guardians', probably the Church Wardens, to care for the homeless within the town. Had it not been for the continual arrival of destitute travellers, these two sanctuaries, plus some generous donations to the special Sunday morning collection of alms, food and clothes, the money provided from various bequests and the tips which travellers left at the inns for the 'poor of this place' might have been sufficient. As it was, these alms had to be spread too thinly and the local poor and distressed suffered because of the needs of the travellers.

The Vagrants

Unfortunately, even more poor travellers came into the town. The closing of the religious houses was a national not just a local event. In some areas land owners were enclosing the common fields, without the legally-applied supervision which was set up in the 18th century, and a number of distressed, confused and often elderly people took to the roads. In addition, periods of severe weather pushed other families below the poverty line. It was all too easy to become what was known as a vagrant.

84 BCRO, Shillington Parish Register.

Bedfordshire was one of many counties which was at risk of being swamped economically by these sad, destitute families and individuals. In 1585 a proclamation was agreed by the Justices of the Peace for Bedfordshire for 'the restraint of Wandering Roges and Vacabounds'. At a meeting held on 19th April they set out 'for the avoiding of Idlenesse and for the reformation of idle evill disposed Roges Vacabounds and other lewde persons . . . the nomber whereof now of late have greatly abounded, and daily more and more doe encrease . . . and great hinderance to the impotent* poore whoes reliefe thereby is taken away . . .'[85].

The recommendations to which the local Justices put their name were the building of what would become known as Houses of Correction or Industry. They ordered that '. . . the inhabitants of . . . every Towne, Village and Hamlet [of this county, shall set] a strong watch and warde kept from sunne setting until next day at night . . .'.

As a result a regular search was to be made for 'Roges, Vagabonds, beggers and other suspicious and unknown persons', these were to be taken before a Justice and sent to the House of Correction and put to work'**. Local people who were entitled to receive alms, itinerant workers or salesmen and men such as disabled soldiers, who were allowed to support themselves by begging, were to apply for the renewal of their licences. The pre-amble to the proclamation sums up Dunstable's position; money which was intended for the care of poor parishioners was needed for even more distressed travellers.

Poor Rates and the Overseers of the Poor

From 1563 an increasing emphasis was put on alms-giving and collection; sermons and plate-rattling were replaced by official collectors, soon to be known as overseers, who were to be elected each year at the Easter meeting of the Parish Vestry. They had to assess the expected needs of the parish for the next twelve months

* Deserving, known to have fallen on hard times.

** This was eventually set up in Bedford in 1629.

85 BCRO, CRT 32.

and then to calculate how this should be spread between the different householders. It was a system similar to, but much simpler than, the modern Community Charge. Money was levied on the value of property with a cut-off point below which payment was not collected. Either the overseer or a paid clerk had to write up the collections and also the expenditure. Where these accounts have survived they are a wonderful source for local historians. Although the early books for Dunstable are missing and those for the 18th century illustrate how much of the money was spent on travellers, Dunstable families in need did receive help.

In the next book we will discover just how complicated the situation became and how greatly the situation was relieved for local people by the generosity of the Marsh family and their descendants.

The Hearth Tax

After the coronation of Charles II a new tax was introduced; lists were made of every house in town, country and isolated hamlet and beside the entry was recorded the number of hearths. This became the basis for collecting the tax – usually two shillings per hearth per year. Although these records are purely lists of householders (not addresses) and hearths they provide a wealth of information.

Smoke was carried away from these hearths by external chimneys which were still comparatively new in Bedfordshire. There were many places where half the houses in the community still had only one hearth and it is of interest to compare this proportion between communities. Another useful comparison is made possible by looking at the proportion of people in each community who for financial reasons were excused from paying the tax. In 1934 Lydia Marshall published The Bedfordshire figures for 1671 and from these we can learn a great deal about Dunstable[86]. To identify the gentry, the innkeepers, beerhouse keepers, post masters*, blacksmiths, saddlers, and others it is

* Those who hired out horses.

86 Marshall, L. BHRS. Vol. 16.

essential to have additional information. In the case of Dunstable we are fortunate to have a wealth of deeds, wills, and other papers which make it possible to link many of the recorded names with their places of business.

Even a cursory look at the Dunstable figures illustrates that there were three inns which were much larger than the very comfortable manor house at Houghton Regis, which had twelve hearths whereas The Bull had eighteen, the White Horse seventeen and The White Hart fifteen. Another useful comparison is that Kingsbury and Priory House, both known to be the homes of 'gentry', each had six hearths. Twelve other buildings had six or more hearths. These were not all inns but the total includes The Three Black Swans, The Sugar Loaf and The Red Lion. The Nags Head and The Windmill (the original Crown) each had five.

During the late 17th century, entrepreneur George Briggs owned six of the inns and beerhouses. His mother was still living in the family house, described as being 'in the westend of Dunstable'*. As one of the largest houses in South Bedfordshire, it had twenty-three hearths (the same number as Someries Castle). Two more interesting facts disclosed by the tax list are that more than half the householders were too poor to pay the tax and about the same proportion of the rest were living in a house with only one hearth. However, there is no evidence of extreme poverty and it seems likely that there was so much skilled, semi-skilled and unskilled work available that most people were able to keep themselves out of the workhouse.

From the 209 houses and inns listed it is possible to calculate a very approximate number of residents. Lydia Marshall uses the accepted figure of 4.8 as an average household size, which would suggest a population of around 1,000**.

---

* The building which now stands on the eastern corner of West Street and Matthew Street is almost definitely the remaining part of this building.

** This figure is higher than that suggested by Lydia Marshall. When examining the original records she found some Dunstable residents linked in pairs and therefore included these single occupancies as 2 households per house.There is no evidence to confirm this.

Celia Fiennes Visits Dunstable.

Late in the summer of 1697 the intrepid traveller, Celia Fiennes, rode into Dunstable travelling south through Northampton, Woburn (where she enjoyed Red Coralina gooseberries) and Hockliffe where she joined the Holyhead Road (A5). The prosperity of the town is confirmed by her description; she notes the 'steepe chaulkly hill' (Puddle hill) on the outskirts of the town and then records:

'[Dunstable] its a good town as you shall meete with on the Road, its full of Inns, there is a long large streete with a great water in the streete it looks like a large pond; here I went to see two of my Relations, Daughters to Sir Charles Wolsley, one marry'd there to a Doctor of Physick Dr Marsh with whom was a maiden sister my Cos'n Bridget Woolsly'.

The Marsh Family of Kingsbury

Celia's cousin by marriage as John Marsh, grandson of the William Marshe, Gent who is described on the family memorial, in the Priory Church, as 'of an ancient family in The Parish of Dunstable'.

Little is known about the once-royal estate of Kingsbury from the mid 16th century until the early 17th. This Marsh family are quite likely to be those who were previously renting land in Caddington and Kensworth. Their eldest son, Daniel, was baptised at the Priory Church on 16th February 1605. Four more sons and two daughters were baptised during the next twenty years, though not all survived. As the first three boys died before their father and the fourth, John, became a well-known local attorney in Leighton Buzzard, it was Francis, the youngest, baptised 28th October 1624, who settled at Kingsbury. He married Elizabeth, daughter of the above George Briggs and their six children were baptised between 1652 and 1664. John Marsh of Leighton Buzzard was included in a list of Bedfordshire Royalists but it seems likely that Francis lived quietly at Kingsbury throughout the Civil War[87]. Although he was around

87 BHRS. Vol. 65.

twenty there are no references to him in connection with either army, nor did he become involved with the problems concerning religion. However, his memorial in the Priory Church clearly records where his sympathies lay, his 'constant piety', his 'inviolable attachment through life to God's altar and worship, constancy towards the English Apostolic church . . .' and also 'his unfailing fidelity, in alas, most depraved times towards his king, the most holy Martyr, that most beneficient of all men, King Charles . . .' It concludes with reference to his 'wonderous charity towards the poor . . .'.

Their third son John, baptised 1658, trained as a physician and married Dorothy Wolsley, with whom there is no record of any children having been produced. Because John was only thirteen in 1671, his father's name appears on the tax list, but as his mother died in 1682 (when he was 24 years old) and his father three years later, it was probably at Kingsbury where John and Dorothy entertained Celia Fiennes.

Dunstable was 'Full of Inns'

As Celia Fiennes approached the Houghton/Dunstable boundary she would have seen the very large and impressive inn called The Bull on her right. At that time it belonged to Henry Earle and was part of the network that he and his partners owned to service their stage coaches, which were by now in competition with many other services. It was a genuine stage coach inn and therefore the provision of hot and cold drinks and food at any hour of the day or night and availability of some of their best accommodation for the use of passengers was expected. What had attracted Henry Earle was the large amount of land connected to The Bull. This was divided into numerous paddocks or 'closes' which were ideal for rearing horses or resting valuable horses recovering from injury. It is interesting to note that many of the Victorian houses in north Dunstable were built on the 'Bull Closes'.

Dunstable's success was that there were inns providing accommodation for every type of traveller – both beerhouses and specialist houses where victuallers supplied both food and drink.

With the Bull behind her, Celia Fiennes would have passed another 14 inns and beerhouses before she turned left into East Street!

Nearly opposite the Bull was a new high-class inn known as The Duke of Bedford's Arms (now the offices of Dunstable Town Council) and almost next to that was The Sugar Loaf, the latter having been built soon after the Restoration but partly rebuilt in 1715. Both of these specialised in the up-market private trade and had space to keep quality horses for hire. However, nearly opposite The Sugar Loaf, The Crown, (sometimes known as The Windmill) which also specialised in the private side of the travel market, was so hemmed-in that ostlers had to take the horses to and from a stable yard and paddocks in South Street. Free standing beside the pond, out in front of the Crown, was one of the forges owned by the Short family. Celia mentioned one long pond but it was portrayed as two in 1762. Earlier in the century Henry Moreton had described his house, next door to The Crown, as The Cock Inn but by 1697 his descendents were describing themselves as 'victuallers', 'collarmakers' or 'saddlers'.

In the 16th century the famous White Horse Inn, where Henry VIII used to stay, included a block of rooms on the southern side of its archway – which adjoined The Raven beer house, now called the Crown, and a long run of buildings on the northern side. By the time of Celia's visit the business next to the Cock, once part of the White Horse, was running as a separate beer house known as 'The Wrestlers'. However, The White Horse was still a respected inn, although the landlord, Henry Sam, may have relied on the hiring out of horses and in his position as 'postmaster' to make up most of his income.*

From at least 1687 Henry Sam is recorded as the Royal Mail's representative in South Bedfordshire. He was responsible for receiving letters from a very wide area, which were then handed into the care of the official post 'boy'. In return, letters were left with him and he had to keep them safely until they were

* Post master is a confusing title. It could be used to describe a man who made his living by keeping horses for hire but increasingly it was used to describe the man who was licensed to handle the Royal Mail.

collected. Originally Sam was paid £25 per year but by the time of his last year, in 1703, he was receiving £40.

On the other side of North Street, the medieval White Hart had been modernised and successfully adapted as a stopping place for stage coaches. There was a blacksmith's forge at the back and, at times, a currier, i.e. a leather worker's yard. On its northern side there was a beer house called The Bear.

Two or three buildings nearer to the crossroads was The Three Black Swans. This *may* have been what was, until recently, Charlie Cole's well known cycle shop, with its elaborate medieval wall painting. The eminent expert, the late Clive Rouse, dated these pictures to around 1600. He queried whether this internal wall had ever been part of an inn. Robert Poole, landlord of The Three Black Swans, had six hearths registered in the 17th century Hearth Tax. His wife Mary was involved in the famous witch scandal of 1666 and a thief was caught there in 1670[88]; otherwise little recorded evidence of this inn has been found. However, the

The bicycle which hung over Charlie Cole's Cycle Shop. This is where the medieval wall paintings were found.

---

88 BCRO, HSA. 1670. W 33–34.

will of John Marsh of Leighton Buzzard refers to eleven cottages which were once connected with Kingsbury Farm, Church Street but adjacent to High Street North[89]. They were described as being on the site of The Three Swans Inne. Further research might identify this site as including and lying behind the present Nationwide Building Society, where the wall paintings are displayed.

The Medieval Wall Paintings

These were found in 1954 in an upstairs room and were in serious need of restoration. In 1985 the Nationwide Building Society bought the building. By this time there was a Victorian front wall which was very unstable. The society paid to have the paintings removed and the walls rebuilt. When the restored pictures were returned they were mounted on a ground floor wall where everyone could see them. The main picture depicts a hunting scene, the huntsman wearing Elizabethan clothes and,

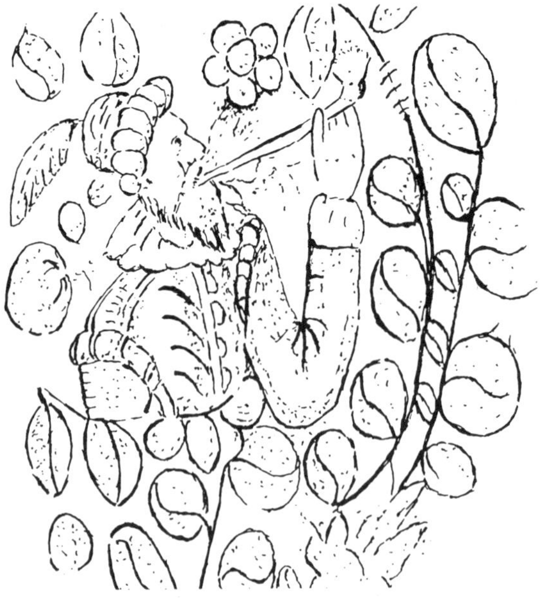

Detail from the hunting scene painted c.1600, now on the wall of the Nationwide Building Society. (Courtesy of Dunstable Town Council.)

89 BCRO, Z. 455/8 also contains this information.

what to the author looks like a horn, is thought to be a pipe. If this is so, it is one of the first representations of pipe-smoking in this country. Trade tokens have been found, dated 1668, with a greyhound carrying a hare, between two crossed tobacco pipes. On one side the name is Daniell Fossey, on the other Dunstable 1668 – HIS HALF PENNY[90].

Originally the scene may have run onto the other walls, but all that remained in 1954 were some narrow panels comprising a pattern of leaves. During the year that Mrs Wendy Mills was mayor, her charity paid to have these restored and mounted in Dunstable library. The deeds of this building do not go back before the 19th century and surprisingly no written records have been found which mention the pictures. Travelling artists of this calibre were expensive and the commission was probably ordered by an innkeeper who expected a high-class trade. A similar but larger example can be seen in a shop which was once part of the White Hart in St. Albans.

There Were Inns in the Middle of the Road!

Celia Fiennes had a lively curiosity and it is a pity that she stayed at her cousin's house and does not describe any of the inns. However, her view of this building may have been obscured by the buildings which stood out in the road; in 1542 they were referred to as being on Whites Lane. There are no reference to this lane after 1600 but it was probably a narrow piece of road between these free-standing buildings and The Three Black Swans and The Red Lion (similar to Ashton Square today), which would allow the stream of traffic to use the wider, western, side.

The 1542 rent list mentions the inns The Lion and The Peacock, a private house and something called a Cokerey (Cook house?). In later centuries they are quite well recorded but as the Eleanor Cross was taken down in the 1640s and at least one house was rebuilt it is difficult to speak with confidence. In the map on page 140 the first building which Celia would have passed was still called The Peacock but when George Briggs made his will in 1692 he described it as a 'dwelling house, called The

90 Benson, N. Dunstable in Detail.

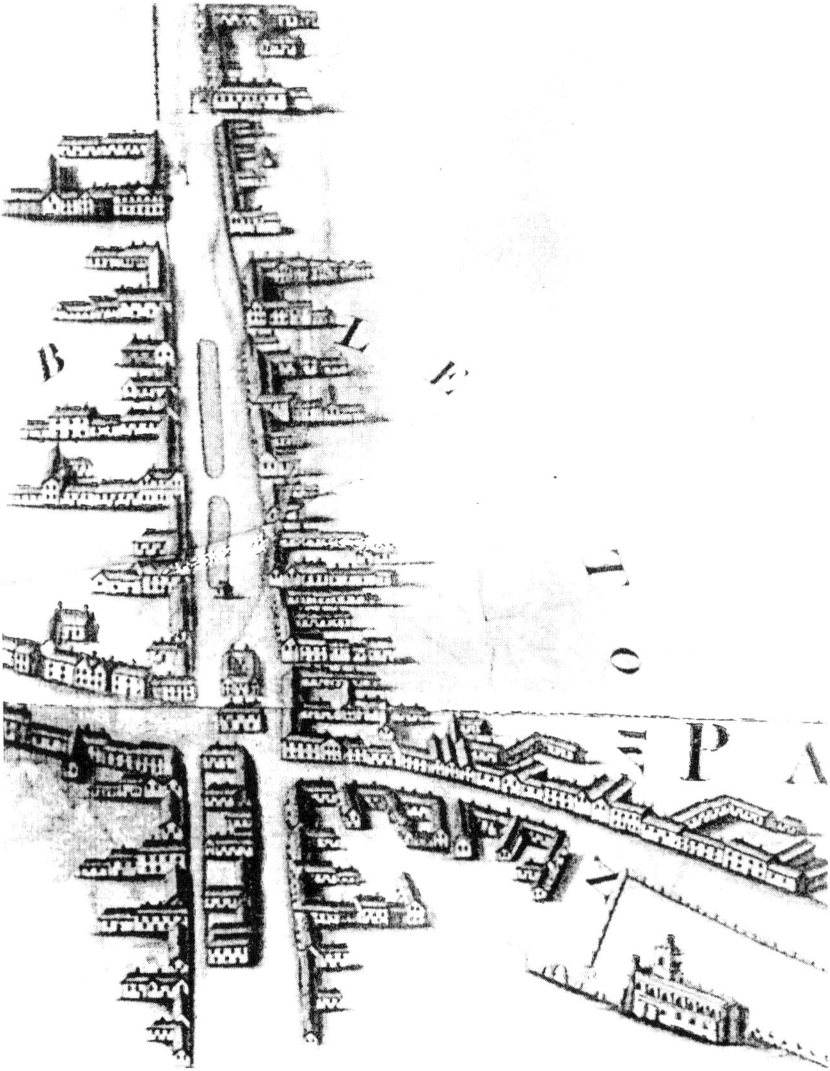

Part of a map produced for the Duke of Bedford in 1766 showing the Town of Dunstable, the ponds, The Lyon, The Peacock, the blacksmith's forge and what may be the 'Court House' standing on the cross roads.

Peacock'[91]. Next to it (and sharing a courtyard) was the tenement which Briggs referred to as The White Lyon. It was then and for some years afterwards occupied by the Cooper family who were probably victuallers. It was inherited by John Platt, the nephew of George Briggs, who, when he made his will in 1708, referred to it as The White Lyon or Cross House. Henry Cooper was the occupier[92]. Included in various lists of quit rent payers* are references to a house which a Richard Fisher had built [in the road] 'against the Red Lion'. A lease to John Duke of Bedford, dated 28th December 1738, mentions a piece of 'waste ground and soyle laying in the markett place being part of the late demolished crosse there together with all the structures as they were then built by Richard Fisher . . .' . . . and to take materials from the old Dominican Friary 'to build and finish' the said house 'to make the same habitable with chambers to the house called the Court House upon the said waste ground in the market place to keep people from the rain'[93]. Richard Fisher was one of the wealthier residents included in a tax assessment list c1628[94].

These buildings would have blocked Celia's view of the well-known Red Lion inn but as she turned left into Church Street she would have ridden right round it. Many readers will remember that it stood out into Church Street until recent times, having apparently been added to the original end of North Street. It was built in the 14th century and for some centuries was known as The White Swan[95]. Probably because the Eleanor Cross and The White Lyon blocked the west wall, the main entrance was in East Street. It had barns at the back which adjoined other barns owned by The King's Head. The Red Lion paddocks were on a rented site in West Street. It is not yet possible to say exactly when the White Swan's name changed to the Red Lion, but it

91 BCRO BS 153.
92 BCRO BS 154.
93 BCRO, E/22/28.
94 BCRO, T53/10.
95 Evans, V. Dunstable With the Priory, 1100–1550.
* People who paid small annual sums to the Lord of the Manor in lieu of what had once been work services.

may have been around 1600. It was already renamed when the Earl of Huntingdon visited in 1639. He recorded his expenses which can be found amongst the Hastings Manuscripts.

He did not make clear if he had more than one servant travelling with him. His room, fire and candles only cost him five shillings (25p) but bread, beer and boiled mutton came to over sixteen shillings (80p). He himself enjoyed: roast mutton, a hen, and a dozen larks, served with salad and lemon juice. This all came to about ten shillings. His wine, sugar and fruit cost over five shillings. His breakfast eggs cost sixpence; he tipped the cook and chambermaid three shillings and sixpence (17 1/2p) and left one shilling and sixpence for the poor. He took three dozen larks with him (four shillings and sixpence) and his bill for supper, bed and breakfast was £2.6s.

And More Inns Elsewhere

The very old public house on the north side of Church Street (east of the Red Lion) is remembered with affection as the White Horse. When Celia Fiennes rode by it was still known as the King's Head.

This is the last inn that she would have passed before reaching Kingsbury but there were of course others in West Street, Middle Row and South Street. The largest and most important of these was The Saracen's Head, an inn which has managed to keep the same name since it was opened before 1500. A detailed account of the known history of each inn will be included in the next book in this series.

Chapter 8

A Century of Change

Publishers of history books who divide up the centuries under a series of descriptive names often refer to the seventeenth as *A Century of Change*. Sticking to purely local issues and not dwelling on the greater issues of fire, plague, international war and the discovery of America it is obvious that the above title would cover the events which took place here in Dunstable. When the book opened, James VI of Scotland was about to become the first Stuart king of England. He was welcomed by groups for all aspects of religious belief and was seen as a

The Nag's Head still proudly stands today, looking out over the busy roundabout. (LPE)

figurehead for reform. So many of these groups were disappointed that England stumbled into civil war. As the book ends, Mary, James's great granddaughter and her Dutch husband William, were bringing in a policy of tolerance and unification.

One inn which still stands today, right in the very centre of the town, has watched over many of the events described in this book. It was also involved in one of the greatest scandles which has ever occurred in Dunstable.

Events in and Around the Nag's Head

There is no reference to an inn on this site during the 16th century. It was possibly opened, or upgraded, by the Settle family, immediately after the Civil War. This would have been in response to the growing travel market.

The complete breakdown of the parish register has been noted in an earlier chapter, also that the first formal entry, after a break of many years, was the request by Josias Settle to have the births of his five children entered retrospectively, also the dates of their baptisms. At the time when many Dunstablians were advocating the baptism of believers, all Settle's children had been baptised (between 1648 and 1657).

The Will of Josias Settle

In 1656 Josias registered the birth of five children but when he made his will 15th June 1666, he only mentioned his wife, Sarah, one son, Jeremiah and his daughter Sarah. Infirm of body but of perfect mind . . . he illustrated his *great belief in God and in the life to come.* He assigned his soul to 'Almighty God my most gracious father in Jesus Christ assuredly believing that my sins are pardoned and salvation purchased for me by and through the all sufficient . . . sufferings of Jesus Christ God and man who died for my sins and rose again . . . and now sitteth at God's right hand'[96].

---

96 BCRO, ABP/W1667/26.

He realised that his body would be buried in the earth but he didn't doubt that 'by the Almighty Power of Jesus Christ' it would be raised again and united with his soul in Glory everlasting. He then set out the division of his temporal estate: 'so that there should be no strife or confusion for or about the same after [his] departure . . .'.

Jeremiah, who was by then nine years old, was to receive the house where Josias was living 'situate and being in Watling Street', known as The Nag's Head, together with the barns and gardens. His smaller house, called The Bell, he left to his sixteen year old daughter Sarah. Until Jeremiah reached the age of twenty-one The Nag's Head was to be managed by his mother. When he came of age he was to pay £40, out of his inheritance, to his sister.

Josias described *The Bell*, which was possibly a beer house, as being in South Street between the inns 'Sarizenshead' and The George. It was let to a shoemaker called William Whitehead.

The long street line of the Saracens Head may be because, in the 18th century, it absorbed what had once been The Bell and The George. (LPE)

From the deeds of the former it seems that these eventually became one inn[97].

In case his wife Sarah remained a widow she was to 'enjoy the profits and benefits' of the inns during her lifetime. She was also to have all the furniture and fittings except in the bedroom known as 'Blue Room'. This was to be kept for daughter Sarah. Josias was buried at the Priory Church on 3rd March 1667. Probably due to the inaccurate registers, Sarah's burial is not recorded.

Elkanah Settle

Josias's eldest son was buried in London in 1724. It may be that one of the reasons Josias requested the registering of the births of his children was because eight-year-old Elkanah was about to go to live with his uncle in Hemel Hempstead.*

In 1666 this uncle paid for him to go to Trinity College Oxford and presumably supported him when he left, without his degree, to follow a career as a playwright in London. Having had a play produced while he was still a student, he must have felt confident of financial success. However, the political and religious unrest of the 1660s and 1670s caused problems of loyalty even within the theatre. As a result his popularity fluctuated and at times he was forced to try out his ideas in a booth at Bartholomew Fair. In 1691 he obtained the appointment of City Poet and the scripts that he wrote for pageants connected with the City, plus play scripts and poems can be seen in the British Library.

In 1674 he married Mary Warner who may have been sister to Sarah's husband John Warner. Nothing is known about their marriage and no children are recorded. Many years later, when his work as a playwright had come to an end, he went to live in

---

* In her book, History of Hemel Hempstead, Susan Yaxley records the activities of a brave and determined Independent couple, John and Margaret Settle. They had a son of their own called Elkanah.

97 I am grateful to the archivist at Whitbread Plc for allowing me to study these deeds.

The Temple of Honour. Part of a cover from one of Settle's pageants staged in 1698.

the London Charter House, with other men of his kind who were referred to as 'poor brothers'. He supported himself by writing poems and letters which could be used as a guide or copy (book) for the less well educated. He died on 12th February 1724 just after his seventy-sixth birthday. The records of his burial have been lost but it may have been at St. Giles in the Fields.

He has been criticised because of fluctuating popularity and the fact that for political reasons he was often held back by the success of Dryden but the list of his productions, his poems, masques and other entertainments, which are listed in Who's Who, are most impressive[98].

The Great Witch Story

Having allowed his eldest son to live with his brother, Josias lived to experience the death of his next two sons.

In the County Record Office is a bundle of sworn statements describing the alarming events which took place in Dunstable in 1665. When we learn that Josias's wife, Sarah, told magistrates that a lady called Elizabeth Pratt said that she had a contract with the devil; that he had promised her that she (Elizabeth) 'should live as well as the best woman in the towne, but that she had found him a liar'; that the devil had appeared to her as a man, as a woman and 'in the likeness of a cat', we know it is going to be a most unusual case!

Sarah's evidence was part of a complicated enquiry into the death of two of her sons. It was their father Josias, who described the sad events to the magistrates, John Vaux of Whipsnade and John Rotherham of Luton. The enquiry took place in August 1666; Settle began by saying that it was at the beginning of Lent, two years before (actually 1665), when Elizabeth Pratt had first come to his house. She had begged Sarah to give her some ale and a little toast, and, while she was waiting, Elizabeth had crossed over to the fire. There she had stroked the head of his sons John (aged 11 years) and Josias (aged 12 years); she said that they were

---

98 Theodorson, G.M. BM. Vol. 2. Brown, F.C. Elkanah Settle – His Life and Work. Kunitz and Haycraft, British Authors before 1800.

her own boys. This took place on a Friday; on the Sunday John 'was tooke with a strange distemper groneing scritching and crying almost continuingly night and day for forty days together until he dyed'. During the final days of this dreadful illness John had torn at his nose and lips and shouted out 'murder, murder, I am bewitched, I am bewitched'!

Josias then went on to describe how two weeks later the elder boy had sickened and that he also had got distressed and cried out just as John had done. 'Ah! Father' [he cried] 'the widow Pratt has bewitched me also'. Whereupon some of the neighbours fetched the said widow Pratt . . .

When they brought Elizabeth into the boys' room his father put a pin into the sick child's hand and told him to scratch her. The poor boy was terrified and lay crying. 'Father I cannot'. So Josias took the pin and tried himself to make the poor old lady bleed but even though he pushed the pin into the veins of her hand, her skin remained dry.

Now this was very serious, because this was one of the ways of recognising a witch. Shortly after this, Settle had accused Elizabeth of witchcraft. She agreed that his sons had been bewitched but said it was nothing to do with her – that it had been two other witches. He told the magistrates that she said there were about twenty witches in Dunstable and that some of them were among the best dressed people in the town! She refused to name the two guilty witches but the town was alive with gossip.

Richard Short remembered that a lady called Ursula Clarke had been to his house and had said that she hoped she could see the end of [a gentleman called William] Metcalfe jun. She had also said 'she had never wished nor craved anything in her life [before] but it came to pass'. Then a man called William Blacknell pointed out that there had been differences between William Metcalfe jun. and Ursula Clarke and that after the difference had been agreed 'Ursula said that she never wished anything in her life but it came to pass and that she hoped to see him, the said Metcalfe, waste like dew against the sun'. It has not been recorded what happened to William Metcalfe's health but financially he must have come near to ruin.

The Metcalfes were one of Dunstable's leading families; they may have been innkeepers, but their main business was keeping horses for hire. In 1619 they paid the quit-rent on The White Horse bowling alley and owed quite high Ship Tax in 1637. We do know who the church wardens were in 1665 and 1666 but a William Metcalfe had been church warden back in 1618 and a later William Metcalfe was one of the church wardens who, after the Civil War, received the register from Thomas Perkins. Metcalfe's story illustrates the mental and spiritual confusion of the 17th century. They were a successful family whose business must have given them the opportunity of meeting the leading people of the day. They were comparatively wealthy, lived in one of Dunstable's larger houses (or a middle-sized inn) and were obviously supporters of the church. Yet when William jun. gave his evidence, the 5th day of August 1666, his story was somewhat bizarre.

He had been alone in his stable yard, with the door and the great gates shut and barred, when he became aware that Elizabeth Pratt was behind him. Convinced that she had come in through the keyhole he called her a witch and ordered her out. Whether he opened the door or whether he had imagined the whole thing we shall never know but he swore on oath that she had bewitched his livestock; as a result sixty-five horses and seventeen pigs had died! Whether Elizabeth was carrying anthrax or whether their deaths were coincidental, a large number of animals must have died. Anthrax causes rapid death in horses but is not so virulent in pigs. Humans are highly resistant but one of the symptoms, if they are infected, is unpleasant sores. These may be what caused the Settle boys so much distress*.

Eventually Elizabeth Pratt named Ursula Clarke and Mary Poole (possibly the wife of Robert of the Three Black Swans) as her accomplices, but by this time two more children were ill. Isabell Chapman, wife of John Chapman (tailor) and Thomas Cooke (husbandman), claimed that they had visited the room where Elizabeth was staying in the Chapman's house and questioned her about two more boys who had been taken ill. She

* I am grateful to Mrs Pat Morgan for pointing out this information.

agreed that they had been bewitched but blamed Mary Poole, Ursula Clarke and Mary Hudson. She also agreed that she had been with others, on the downs, when two meetings had been held, 'standing mid-way between the three knolls'. They had discussed how they should go about bewitching the children but she had not taken part in the actual bewitching'.

The father of the children was Thomas Heywood*; he said that Elizabeth Pratt had told him that Mary Hudson had 'tyed a knott of black wool, which was bewitched, into the boulster of [his] sick child; as a result his wife had opened the boulster, on which the sick child lay, and had found a knott of wool tyed together' (presumably in some sinister design). She realised the seriousness of the situation, especially as the Settle boys had died, so she sent for George Briggs (the entrepreneur)** and Elizabeth and Mary Metcalfe to witness what she had found.

It is interesting to note that there are no references to Dr Crawley, who by this time had probably arrived in Dunstable, or to any other physician. Even if they had known that the boys were suffering from a severe illness (and not witchcraft) there was nothing that a 17th century doctor could have done.

John Settle was buried at the Priory Church on March 7th 1665, Thomas Heywood on March 29th and his seven year old brother, John, on the 12th day of April. The burial of Josias Settle has not been recorded but once again the original pages of the register are missing.

Something Must be Done

There are references to Elizabeth Pratt being 'under restraint' and it seems likely that she was eventually kept under house arrest at John Chapman's house. We can imagine that, even before the deaths of the second pair of brothers, the town must have been in an uproar. Apart from the local distress and panic the innkeepers would have tried most desperately to prevent the locals and the servants from gossiping to their guests. Nobody wanted the story

---

* There are several different spellings.

** In 1692 he, or his son, left bequests to George Settle, John and Robert Warner, three of Josias Settle's grandchildren.

of a strange sickness, which killed both boys and horses, being carried up and down the Holyhead road and certainly not tales of witchcraft! Although the 'Witch Finder General' had eventually been discredited back in 1647, nearly twenty years later in Dunstable, rich and poor alike still believed in witchcraft[99].

Even the Local Magistrates Believed in Witchcraft

Once the first of the Heywood boys died, the whole story was reported to the local magistrates. On the 4th of April they ordered a committee of ladies to examine the bodies of the suspects for witchmarks. The resulting statement was signed by the mothers of the dead boys, Mary Metcalfe and nine others. They reported that:

1. On Ursula Clarke they had found nothing – 'she is as other women are' and that 'she said the Lord's prayer'.
2. Upon Mary Poole they had found 'a peece of flesh upon her left shoulder and an impression in the middle of her back and that she hath a blew spott like a mole within the sydes of her privityes'.
3. On Mary Hudson 'they found two little short teath in her private place'.

They made a separate statement about Elizabeth Pratt, who by this time was talking even more wildly and they had no trouble at all in convincing themselves that she was a witch. In one rash statement she had inferred that a George Heywood was also working with the devil and that his back became a panel for her to ride on and she 'had ridden him up hill and down hill'.

When she was called in front of the magistrates Elizabeth blamed the other three. She then said that the devil had appeared to her in the form of a cat and that he had 'commanded' her to go up on the Downs with the others and plan the bewitching of the Heywood boys. Whether the magistrates seriously believed all this we do not know, but something had to be done. They ordered that three of the ladies should be sent to Bedford Gaol to await the next visit by the judges.

---

99 Evans, V. Folk.

It is probably lucky for Elizabeth Pratt that she died before the arrival of the judges. They would have had no choice but to find this confused and deluded old lady guilty of witchcraft. As it was the other two appear to have escaped without a trial[100].

Back at the Nag's Head

Josias Settle had described himself as 'infirm' when he made his will in June 1666. He was buried on March 3rd 1667 and the Nag's Head was licensed in the name of 'Widow Settle'. Her daughter, Sarah, came of age on October 23rd 1670 and married John Warner the following April 10th. He came from a family with a similar background of barber surgeons. The Nag's Head was still registered in the name of 'Widow Settle' in 1671 but the date of her death is not recorded. However, it seems likely, as Jeremiah wouldn't be twenty-one for another eight years, that John and Sarah took over the Nag's Head together with his 'care and education' as required in the will.

Once she was twenty-one Sarah became legal owner of The Bell. It may have had a very low rental value because by the end of 1672 they had decided to sell it. The final papers for the sale, to Thomas Chapman, barber, were signed on the 14th January 1673[101].

Jeremiah was twenty-one on November 22nd 1678 but no records have been found until his marriage, at Luton, in 1679. His wife was Elizabeth Dyre and she also appears to have been a member of a family of innkeepers/barbers. By the time that their son, George, was born, nine months later, the family was settled at Woburn.

What financial arrangements or settlements had been made between Jeremiah, Sarah and her husband are not known, but in 1696 Jeremy Settle, barber/surgeon of Woburn, received £40 from John Warner*. At that time John Warner, barber/surgeon, was

---

* This is confusing because the Jeremiah who was buried at Dunstable in 1681 has always been considered to be the brother of Sarah.

100 The order of events in the above story are not necessarily in the correct order but are strictly based on BRCO, HSA. 1671 W.

101 BCRO, AD. 770.

living at the Nag's Head; it was described as standing 'east upon Watling Street, south upon the Icknield Way and north upon the house of Edward Chester'. By the end of the year an F Warner, barber/surgeon of Berkhamsted, invested money in the business.

One of the characteristics of the 17th century was the very high death rate and this also can be illustrated by looking at the life of the Settle family. During the 1670s and 1680s John Warner lost his wife and several of his children. The eldest, John (jun.) died in 1698 and it appears that when John himself died, in 1702, Elkanah was the only surviving member of the Settle family.

Whether he came to Dunstable we do not know, but according to the deeds, on the 21st September 1722, a document was drawn up for Elkanah to convey the property to George Knowles who had opened a large drapery shop next door. They signed the document two days later and the family connection had ended.

Both the Nag's Head and Dunstable were moving on into a new decade and we will follow their progress in the next book in the series.

Who Was Running 17th Century Dunstable?

The above events took place long before Dunstable had either a mayor or a town council. It is interesting to note that when there was a crisis the people turned for advice to respected businessmen and their families. They then consulted the magistrates who took statements and referred the matter to a higher court at Bedford.

As we have seen, the officers who were responsible for the care of the poor and sick and also for the maintenance of the roads were elected at the Easter Vestry Meeting. George Briggs and William Metcalfe may have been church wardens in 1666 but those pages of the register have not survived.

Priory House

Apart from the Marsh and Briggs families, the other influential family was the Crawleys at Priory House. During the Civil War, the three sons of Judge Sir Francis Crawley of Someries, Luton, were ardent Royalists. After the war his youngest son, Robert, married Joane Taverner of Hexton and moved into Priory House. He had probably trained as an army doctor, being styled Robert Crawley MD when he was buried at Kensworth, in 1697, by his friend the Rev. John Lord. He bequeathed £1 each to his children and his mansion at the south end of Dunstable, together with '5 acres called by the name Pryory' to his wife Joane. She was buried at Kensworth five years later and left the mansion and land to their son John*. Both John and his son Thomas trained and practised as doctors, the latter becoming a respected specialist in the discipline of mental illness, using some of the rooms at Priory House for the treatment of his private patients.

The Manor House

Although these three families were respected and comparatively wealthy, they were never Lords of the Manor. This position was leased from the Crown first by the Earls of Ailesbury (Houghton

The Manor House in 1870 with the 'old' post office, now the Social Security Office, on the right.

* The deeds of Priory House are in the possession of Dunstable Town Council.

House) and later by the Dukes of Bedford. In 1870 the market fairs and certain pieces of land were bought from Queen Victoria by Dunstable Council.

The so-called Manor House stood in High Street North where the modern 'former' post office building stands today, south of the 'old' post office (now the D.S.S.). By 1840 it was a private house in the ownership of Edward Burr, the Duke's steward hiring rooms at the Sugar Loaf when he came to visit his tenants. However, it may originally have been built to house a steward. When Zachary Symmes came to Dunstable he arranged an eighteen year lease on the manor-house, formerly called The Angell, now called The Stone House[102]. This reference, however, leads to confusion. Over the centuries, several different houses, including the one at the southern corner of Albion Road and High Street South, had been referred to by that name.*

The first surviving manor court roll starts in 1743 but it can be assumed that the meetings were very similar in the late 17th century[103].

The Manor Court

The Duke's 'gentleman steward' was in charge, assisted by twelve local jurors plus foreman and two affeerors who traditionally helped to assess the fines. If anyone was serving for the first time, he would have to buy a shilling's-worth of ale to be shared with his companions. First it was agreed to continue with the existing bye-laws and then small fines were registered and collected from any new tenants. Other 'fines' which had actually become mutually-accepted rents were concerned with the 'Lord's waste'. Any small piece of ground (other than the main roads or a measured and recognised piece in private ownership or tenancy) was regarded as the property of the Lord of the Manor. The fine for grazing tethered cows on the grass

---

102 BCRO AD 907
103 BCRO BOR DV 5/1.
* I am grateful to Mrs Joan Curran for showing me the results of her research into the history of this building.

verges was five shillings. Innkeepers who erected signposts out in the road were fined one shilling, as were the owners of houses with porches. Anyone enclosing a yard, garden or orchard was fined slightly more, while those infilling or building houses along the edge of the road were fined several shillings. Some items, e.g. positioning woodpiles and manure heaps well away from the roads, went back to the original bye-laws of the early 13th century. Before the court closed, four constables, two ale-tasters, two men to check the quality of leather that was sold and a hayward (whose job was to ensure the good repair of hedges and ditches) were elected.

The Market

The end of High Street North which adjoins the present roundabout was once on a slope and was known as Market Hill. This was where the main stalls were laid out; the cattle-market was in the Square and the sheep-market was in West Street. It is not known exactly what goods were on sale but the currier (leather dresser) who worked behind the White Hart had a stall and no doubt there were stalls selling straw and plait in addition to singing birds in cages and larks (netted on the Downs) prepared for the table. Everything was strictly controlled by the traditional rules of the Manor Court. Anyone who hawked or pitched in the market had to pay one penny or, if at the fair, two pennies. Those selling out of a hamper had to pay a rent of one penny, whereas those using a basket only had to pay a halfpenny.

Newcomers wanting a stall had to pay an entry fee of ten shillings and all stall-holders had to pay tolls. For every horse or bull that was sold the toll was four pence, for every cow two pence and every calf, hog or pig one penny. Sheep and lambs, however, were charged at eight pence for twenty. An important rule for any market was the strict supervision of weights and measures. At each sitting of the 'Manor Court' it was recorded that every stall-holder had to check their equipment against the standard provided.

The Borough of Dunstable, Imperial Half Gallon measure 1868. (LPE)

A collection of standard weights and measures used in Dunstable market in 1868. (LPE)

The Straw Hat Industry

Nothing has been said in this book about the people noted in 1681 by Thomas Baskerville as being 'very curious in making straw hats and other works of that nature'. There are very few written records before 1700 but behind the noise and bustle of the travel industry there must have been a rapidly expanding hat industry. When the feltmakers succeeded in bringing a bill before Parliament, in 1689, to enforce the wearing of woollen winter hats, a local petition, said to represent nearly one thousand families, was presented against it. It claimed that fourteen thousand people were dependent on the industry and covered an area including Luton, Dunstable and twelve villages between Sundon and Redbourne and across to Edlesborough[104]. It was

The white, bay windowed building (Brown Ltd. and Bata) was, up to the coming of the railways, The Crown Inn. It then went bankrupt but soon reopened as The Crown Hat Factory.

104 Dony, J. A History of the Straw Hat Industry.

obviously an industry manned from family labour and may have included the making of toys, fancy goods and bottle sleeves as well as hats. When there was a similar petition thirty years later, the area included had spread across to Leighton Buzzard and south to St. Albans, but it was still a cottage industry and had not yet attracted wealthy entrepreneurs from outside the area. These would come to Dunstable just in time to save a collapse in employment when the arrival of the railway brought the stage and mail coach industry to an abrupt end.

One again the people of Dunstable made a rapid adjustment. This time from hotels to hat, or rather bonnet, making. They were successful once again!

Background Sources

We are extremely lucky to have available so many records and documents published by the Bedfordshire Historical Record Society. A detailed topography following the dissolution, wills, inventories, causes and events during the Civil War, the struggle for freedom of worship, the early Baptist minute books – plus helpful background explanations, the baptising of the sheep and many other subjects are covered in these volumes. The history of the local Quakers, a short biography of Elkanah Settle, the problem of poor and sick travellers and many other subjects can, by using the index prepared by Yvonne Nicholls, be found in the volumes of the *Bedfordshire Magazine*. The pamphlets published under the general title Elstow Moot Hall leaflets are particularly useful for the period of the Civil War.

Miss Patricia Bell's *Belief in Bedfordshire* explains the background to the religious controversy right across the county. Nigel Benson's *Dunstable in Detail* gives a short but accurate history of each building in the centre of Dunstable and the small booklet, *For the Next Generation*, by Reg Baker is a useful record of the Ebenezer Chapel.

The various travellers' tales and most of the other books quoted can be found in the Special Collection of the Harpur Street Library, Bedford.

INDEX

Buildings and Other Locations

Books Published by THE BOOK CASTLE

COUNTRYSIDE CYCLING IN BEDFORDSHIRE, BUCKINGHAMSHIRE AND HERTFORDSHIRE: Mick Payne.
Twenty rides on- and off-road for all the family. 1 871199 92 1

PUB WALKS FROM COUNTRY STATIONS:
Bedfordshire and Hertfordshire: Clive Higgs.Fourteen circular country rambles, each starting and finishing at a railway station and incorporating a pub-stop at a mid-way point. 1 871199 53 0

PUB WALKS FROM COUNTRY STATIONS:
Buckinghamshire and Oxfordshire: Clive Higgs.
Circular rambles incorporating pub-stops. 1 871199 73 5

LOCAL WALKS: North and Mid Bedfordshire: Vaughan Basham.
Twenty-five thematic circular walks. 1 871199 48 4

FAMILY WALKS: Chilterns South: Nick Moon.
Thirty 3 to 5 mile circular walks. 1 871199 38 7

FAMILY WALKS: Chilterns North: Nick Moon.
Thirty shorter circular walks. 1 871199 68 9

CHILTERN WALKS: Hertfordshire, Bedfordshire and North Buckinghamshire: Nick Moon. 1 871199 13 1
CHILTERN WALKS: Buckinghamshire: Nick Moon. 1 871199 43 3
CHILTERN WALKS: Oxfordshire and West Buckinghamshire: Nick Moon. 1 871199 08 5
A trilogy of circular walks, in association with the Chiltern Society. Each volume contains 30 circular walks.

OXFORDSHIRE WALKS: Oxford, the Cotswolds and the Cherwell Valley: Nick Moon. 1 871199 78 6
OXFORDSHIRE WALKS: Oxford, the Downs and the Thames Valley: Nick Moon. 1 871199 32 8
Two volumes that complement Chiltern Walks: Oxfordshire and complete coverage of the county, in association with the Oxford Fieldpaths Society. Thirty circular walks in each.

JOURNEYS INTO BEDFORDSHIRE: Anthony Mackay.
Foreword by The Marquess of Tavistock, Woburn Abbey. A lavish book of over 150 evocative ink drawings. 1 871199 17 4

JOURNEYS INTO BUCKINGHAMSHIRE: Anthony Mackay
Superb line drawings plus background text: large format landscape gift book. 1 871199 14 X

BUCKINGHAMSHIRE MURDERS: Len Woodley
Nearly two centuries of nasty crimes. 1 871199 93 X

HISTORIC FIGURES IN THE BUCKINGHAMSHIRE LANDSCAPE: John Houghton.
Major personalities and events that have shaped the county's past, including a special section on Bletchley Park. 1 871199 63 8

TWICE UPON A TIME: John Houghton. 1 871199 09 3
Short stories loosely based on fact, set in the North Bucks area.

MANORS and MAYHEM, PAUPERS and PARSONS: Tales from Four Shires: Beds., Bucks., Herts., and Northants.: John Houghton
Little-known historical snippets and stories. 1 871199 18 2

MYTHS and WITCHES, PEOPLE and POLITICS: Tales from Four Shires: Bucks., Beds., Herts., and Northants.: John Houghton.
Anthology of strange, but true historical events. 1 871199 82 4

FOLK: Characters and Events in the History of Bedfordshire and Northamptonshire: Vivienne Evans.
Anthology about people of yesteryear – arranged alphabetically by village or town. 1 871199 25 5

JOHN BUNYAN: His Life and Times: Vivienne Evans.
Highly-praised and readable account. 1 871199 87 5

THE RAILWAY AGE IN BEDFORDSHIRE: Fred Cockman.
Classic, illustrated account of early railway history. 1 871199 22 0

GLEANINGS REVISITED: Nostalgic Thoughts of a Bedfordshire Farmer's Boy: E W O'Dell. 1 871199 77 8
His own sketches and early photographs adorn this lively account of rural Bedfordshire in days gone by.

FARM OF MY CHILDHOOD, 1925–1947: Mary Roberts.
An almost vanished lifestyle on a remote farm near Flitwick. 1 871199 50 6

BEDFORDSHIRE'S YESTERYEARS Vol 2: The Rural Scene: Brenda Fraser-Newstead. 1 871199 47 6
Vivid first-hand accounts of country life two or three generations ago.

BEDFORDSHIRE'S YESTERYEARS Vol 3: Craftsmen and Tradespeople: Brenda Fraser-Newstead.
Fascinating recollections over several generations practising many vanishing crafts and trades. 1 871199 03 4

BEDFORDSHIRE'S YESTERYEARS Vol 4:
War Times and Civil Matters: Brenda Fraser-Newstead.
Two World Wars, plus transport, law and order, etc. 1 871199 23 9

DUNNO'S ORIGINALS: Facsimile of 1821–2:
Little-known part of Dunstable's heritage. Anthology of prose, poetry, legend. New introduction by John Lunn. 1 871199 19 0

DUNSTABLE IN TRANSITION: 1550–1700:
Vivienne Evans. 1 871199 98 0
Wealth of original material as the town evolves without the Priory.

DUNSTABLE WITH THE PRIORY: 1100–1550: Vivienne Evans.
Dramatic growth of Henry I's important new town around a major crossroads. 1 871199 56 5

DUNSTABLE DECADE: THE EIGHTIES:
A Collection of Photographs:
Pat Lovering. 1 871199 35 2
A souvenir book of nearly 300 pictures of people and events in the 1980s.

DUNSTABLE IN DETAIL: Nigel Benson. 09509773 2 2
A hundred of the town's buildings and features, plus town trail map.

OLD DUNSTABLE: Bill Twaddle.
A new edition of this collection of early photographs. 1 871199 05 0

BOURNE and BRED: A Dunstable Boyhood Between the Wars:
Colin Bourne.
An elegantly written, well-illustrated book capturing the spirit of the town over fifty years ago. 1 871199 40 9

ROYAL HOUGHTON: Pat Lovering: 0 9509773 1 4
Illustrated history of Houghton Regis from the earliest times to the present.

THE STOPSLEY BOOK: James Dyer.
Definitive, detailed account of this historic area of Luton. 150 rare photographs. h/b – 1 871199 24 7; p/b – 1 871199 04 2

THE CHANGING FACE OF LUTON: An Illustrated History:
Stephen Bunker, Robin Holgate and Marian Nichols.
Luton's development from earliest times to the present busy industrial town. Illustrated in colour and mono.
h/b – 1 871199 66 2; p/b – 1 871199 71 9

THE MEN WHO WORE STRAW HELMETS:
Policing Luton, 1840–1974: Tom Madigan.
Meticulously chronicled history; dozens of rare photographs; author served in Luton Police for fifty years. h/b – 1 871199 81 6; p/b – 1 871199 11 5

BETWEEN THE HILLS:
The Story of Lilley, a Chiltern Village:
Roy Pinnock. 1 871199 02 6
A priceless piece of our heritage – the rural beauty remains but the customs and way of life described here have largely disappeared.

KENILWORTH SUNSET:
A Luton Town Supporter's Journal:
Tim Kingston.
Frank and funny account of football's ups and downs. 1 871199 83 2

A HATTER GOES MAD!:
Kristina Howells. 1 871199 58 1
Luton Town footballers, officials and supporters talk to a female fan.

LEGACIES: Tales and Legends of Luton and the North Chilterns:
Vic Lea.
Twenty-five mysteries and stories based on fact, including Luton Town Football Club. Many photographs. 1 8711199 91 3

LEAFING THROUGH LITERATURE:
Writers' Lives in Hertfordshire and Bedfordshire: David Carroll.
Illustrated short biographies of many famous authors and their connections with these counties. 1 871199 01 8

A PILGRIMAGE IN HERTFORDSHIRE: H M Alderman.
Classic, between-the-wars tour round the county, embellished with line drawings. 1 871199 33 6

SUGAR MICE AND STICKLEBACKS:
Childhood Memories of a Hertfordshire Lad: Harry Edwards
Vivid evocation of those gentler pre-war days in an archetypal village, Hertingfordbury. 1 871199 88 3

SWANS IN MY KITCHEN: Lis Dorer.
Story of a Swan Sanctuary near Hemel Hempstead. 1 871199 62 X

THE HILL OF THE MARTYR:
An Architectural History of St. Albans Abbey: Eileen Roberts.
Scholarly and readable chronological narrative history of Hertfordshire and Bedfordshire's famous cathedral. Fully illustrated with photographs and plans. h/b – 1 871199 21 2; p/b – 1 871199 26 3

CHILTERN ARCHAEOLOGY: RECENT WORK:
A Handbook for the Next Decade:
edited by Robin Holgate.
The latest views, results and excavations by twenty-three leading archaeologists throughout the Chilterns. 1 871199 52 2

THE TALL HITCHIN SERGEANT:
A Victorian Crime Novel Based on Fact: Edgar Newman.
Mixes real police officers and authentic background with an exciting storyline. 1 871199 07 7

THE TALL HITCHIN INSPECTOR'S CASEBOOK:
A Victorian Crime Novel Based on Fact: Edgar Newman.
Worthies of the time encounter more archetypal villains. 1 871199 67 0

SPECIALLY FOR CHILDREN

VILLA BELOW THE KNOLLS: A Story of Roman Britain:
Michael Dundrow.
An exciting adventure for young John in Totternhoe and Dunstable two thousand years ago. 1 871199 42 5

THE RAVENS: One Boy Against the Might of Rome:
James Dyer. 1 871199 60 3
On the Barton Hills and in the south-east of England as the men of the great fort of Ravensburgh (near Hexton) confront the invaders.

Books Distributed by THE BOOK CASTLE

Pictorial Guide to Bedfordshire	Meadows / Larkman	0900804 10 6
Old Bedfordshire	Houfe	0900804 15 7
The Story of Bedford	Godber	0900804 24 6
Pictorial Guide to Hertfordshire	Meadows	0900804 22 x
The Story of St. Albans	Toms	0900804 28 9
History of Milton Keynes, vol 1	Markham	0900804 29 7
History of Milton Keynes, vol 2	Markham	0900804 30 0
Old Aylesbury	Viney / Nightingale	0900804 21 1
Village Schooldays and Beyond, 1906–23	Chapman	09518217 1 7
Claydon	Chapman	09518217 0 9

Further titles are in preparation.

All the above are available via any bookshop, or from the publisher and bookseller,

THE BOOK CASTLE
12 Church Street, Dunstable, Bedfordshire, LU5 4RU
Tel: (01582) 605670